Scholastic TREASURY OF QUOTATIONS FOR CHILDREN

I quote others to better express myself.

Michel de Montaigne (1533–1592)

Scholastic

TREASURY OF QUOTATIONS FOR CHILDREN

ADRIENNE BETZ

SCHOLASTIC
REFERENCE

Excerpts from *Oh, The Places You'll Go* by Dr. Seuss. Copyright © 1990 by the order of S. Geisel and Audrey Geisel. All rights reserved. Reprinted by permission of Random House, Inc.

"The Kitten" by Ogden Nash from *Verses From 1929 On* by Ogden Nash. Copyright © 1940 by the Curtis Publishing Company. Reprinted by permission of Little, Brown and Co.

Excerpts from "My People" by Langston Hughes in *The Selected Poems of Langston Hughes.* Copyright © 1959 by Langston Hughes; copyright © renewed 1987 by George Houston Bass. Reprinted by permission of Alfred A. Knopf, Inc.

Excerpts from "Dreams" by Langston Hughes in *The Dream Keeper and Other Poems* by Langston Hughes. Copyright © 1932 by Alfred A. Knopf, Inc.; copyright © renewed 1960 by Langston Hughes. Reprinted by permission of Alfred A. Knopf, Inc.

Excerpts from "The Four Corners of the Universe" by Claire R. Farrer in *Singing for Life, the Mescalero Apache Puberty Ceremony,* from *Southwestern Indian Ritual Drama.* Published by the University of New Mexico Press. Used by permission.

"The Entire World" from *Mandan and Hidatsa Music.* Published in B.A.E. (Bureau of American Ethnology) Bulletin 80, copyright © 1923. Reprinted by permission of the Smithsonian Institution Press.

From "Stopping by Woods on a Snowy Evening" from *Complete Poems of Robert Frost.* Copyright 1930, 1939; copyright © 1956, 1958 by Robert Frost; copyright © 1967 by Lesley Frost Ballentine. By permission of Henry Holt and Company.

Library of Congress Cataloging-in-Publication Data

Scholastic treasury of quotations for children/[compiled and written] by Adrienne Betz
    p.   cm.
   Includes index.
   Summary: Presents 1,200 quotations from ancient to modern times on topics such as cooperation, growing up, nature, success, and faith.
   ISBN 0-590-27146-6
   1. Quotations, English. [1. Quotations.] I. Betz, Adrienne.
PN6081.S36   1998   97-34153
082—DC21   CIP
                                                AC

10 9 8 7 6 5 4   02 03

Printed in the U.S.A. 23
First printing, September 1998

Book Design by Nancy Sabato
Typesetting by Brad Walrod

Table of Contents

Introduction

For centuries, literate people kept notebooks in which they copied sentences and passages from the books they read and the speeches and sermons they heard. It was their way of keeping close at hand the quotations they found especially meaningful. They could reread them for inspiration and pass them on to others.

In 1855, a Massachusetts bookseller named John Bartlett published a collection of quotations based on his own commonplace books. Since his collection reflected his tastes and the times in which he lived, most of his quotations came from the Bible, the works of Shakespeare, and other classic British writers. He called his book *Familiar Quotations* because he wanted to show people that many important ideas and phrases that were popular in the English and American culture of his time were not new.

Since 1855, many books of quotations have been published. Most were collected to serve specific purposes, such as providing a reference tool for scholars, or to help ministers and speakers find just the right quotations to use in their speeches. The *Scholastic Treasury of Quotations for Children* is different from Bartlett's and other books because it is for you.

This book reflects what you read in school, what you do at home with your friends and family, and the world you live in today. The 1,200 quotations in this book span the centuries from ancient times to the present and come from many nations. There are quotations that will help you understand the personalities and achievements of great figures from history. There are quotations that reveal how people seem to have the same ideas, problems, and feelings no matter where or when they have lived. Some of the quotations in this book will inspire you, others will make you laugh—and within these pages you are sure to find more than a few quotations that suit you so well that you will remember them and pass them on to others.

> ❝ **W**hat is well said by another is mine.
> SENECA (C. 4 B.C.–A.D. 65)

USING QUOTATIONS IN YOUR OWN SPEAKING AND WRITING

Almost everyone who has ever had to write a speech or a report has had times when it was difficult to find just the right words. One way that authors and speakers have found the right words to express their own ideas is by borrowing or building on quotations.

Introduce an Idea

Getting started is often the hardest part of any writing project.

Many public speakers and professional writers have found that starting out with a quotation provides a great way to introduce an idea to build on as they get ready to present their own thoughts.

Arthur Ashe was a tennis champion who also became an accomplished speaker. In 1990, he spoke at the graduation ceremonies at Kean College in New Jersey and began his speech by quoting from a writer whose work he had read during his own college days:

> **W**hen I was in college in the sixties, my generation's favorite writer/poet/ philosopher was Hermann Hesse. . . . Hesse has a poem entitled "Stages." The first line read, "There is magic in new beginnings." That is what you are doing today: starting over again. Your happiness is deserved.

Describe a Person, Place, or Concept

In 1964, Robert Kennedy was asked to provide an introduction for a special memorial edition of *Profiles in Courage*, written in 1956 by President John F. Kennedy. Robert Kennedy wanted his introduction to pay tribute to his brother and his own kind of courage. Here is how he used a quotation to tell the world about his own brother:

As Andrew Jackson said, 'One man with courage makes a majority.'
That is the effect President Kennedy had on others.

Add Authority and Support Your Opinions

Quoting from an expert in a certain field or from a source respected for its wisdom and authority adds power to any point you are trying to make.

Abraham Lincoln was a great speaker. He had to choose his words carefully as he searched for ways to bring a divided nation together. In his speeches, he frequently used biblical quotations that were known to his audience to support his opinions. Here is how he used a biblical quotation (Mark 3:25) in a speech he gave in 1858:

A house divided against itself cannot stand. I believe this government cannot endure permanently half slave and half free. I do not expect the Union to be dissolved—I do not expect the house to fall—but I do expect that it will cease to be divided. It will become all one thing or all the other.

Find a Title

Borrowing titles from old proverbs and other literary works is a very common practice. Shakespeare used an old proverb as the title for his play *All's Well That Ends Well*, and many modern authors have taken their titles from lines from Shakespeare's works.

Lorraine Hansberry was a gifted author who often made reference to poems she loved in her own plays, speeches, and essays. The title of her play *A Raisin in the Sun* comes from a line from a poem by Langston Hughes, and she included the poem in the introduction to the play to make sure that the meaning of the title was clear to her readers.

Twist a Quotation to Make a Point That People Will Remember

Some of the most effective uses of quotations come from the novel ways people have found to show that they disagree with a famous quotation or familiar proverb.

In 1848, Elizabeth Cady Stanton and Lucretia Mott organized the first national women's rights convention. At this Seneca Falls meeting they presented a Declaration of Sentiments and Resolutions. They carefully chose their words to show how they would have changed the Declaration of Independence:

> We hold these truths to be self-evident,
> that all men *and women* are created equal....

At one time almost every schoolchild learned to recite a poem called "If" by the British poet Rudyard Kipling. In his poem Kipling says "If you can keep your head while all about you are losing theirs...yours is the world and everything that's in it,/And—what's more—you'll be a man my son." In 1957, in a book called *Please Don't Eat the Daisies,* humorist Jean Kerr twisted Kipling's familiar words to present her own point of view:

> If you can keep your head when all about you are losing theirs,
> it's just possible you have not grasped the situation.

Use a Favorite Quotation as a Model to Add Style and Energy to Your Own Words

Quotable people know how to put words together. They can say a lot in a few words and they craft sentences that use different kinds of word patterns to make what they say memorable and pleasing to the ear. You can do the same thing when you write your own sentences.

Here are some examples of famous quotations that use repetition of sounds and words to help make their points:

Ask not what your country can do for you,
ask what you can do for your country.
JOHN F. KENNEDY (1917–1963)

Nothing succeeds like success.
ALEXANDRE DUMAS (1802–1870)

Your children need your presence more than your presents.
JESSE JACKSON (B. 1941)

We have nothing to fear but fear itself.
FRANKLIN D. ROOSEVELT (1882–1945)

Be less curious about people and more curious about ideas.
MARIE CURIE (1867–1934)

Many clever quotations use comparisons and imagery to stimulate your senses and help you think of familiar things in new ways:

Let poetry be like a key
Opening a thousand doors.
VICENTE HUIDOBRO (1893–1948)

There is . . . no Shark like hatred.
DHAMMAPADDA (C. 3RD CENTURY)

Life is something like a trumpet.
If you don't put anything into it, you don't get anything out.
W.C. HANDY (1873–1958)

What images, sensations and feelings do these comparisons suggest to you? What comparisons would you use? What do you have to say about poetry? hatred? about life?

Finding Quotations in This Book

There are three ways you can find a quotation in this book. You can use the table of contents to search by topic, use the index to find quotations by a specific person, or just browse through the main part of the book and see what interests you as you skim through the pages.

Using the Table of Contents

The table of contents provides an alphabetical list of 76 topics. Scan the list to find the topic or topics closest to what you are searching for. For example, if you want to find a quote about baseball, go to page 154 and look through the quotes under the heading Sports. You may also want to see what is listed under topics that relate to opposite concepts. For example, if you want to find quotations about War you might also look under Peace.

Reading Through Each Section

Within each section, the quotations are organized alphabetically by the contributor's last name to help you skim through and find the names of people you may know. Some sections also include special boxes that provide more information about important quotations and the people who said them. Cross references are provided at the end of some sections to point out other topics that contain related quotations.

Using the Biographical Index

If you have found a quote that interests you and you want to know more about who said it, use the index to find out a little bit more about that person and where to find other quotations by that person in the book.

If you are searching for a quotation by a specific person, the index is the first place you should look.

As John Bartlett realized back in 1855, quotations are an important part of our shared heritage and history. When you turn this page you will discover words that have inspired people in the past through difficult times and led to changes that made history. Some of these words and ideas will be familar to you. Others will be new and will challenge you to form new opinions of your own. You may find that as you grow and change, your thoughts about some quotations will change. This is a book filled with ideas for you to read, rediscover, and share again and again.

> **I**mitation is the sincerest of flattery.
> CHARLES CALEB COLTON (1780–1832)

ABOUT THE QUOTATIONS IN THIS BOOK

Each of the quotations in this book was selected because it says a great deal in a few words. In some cases, meanings and additional notes are provided to explain familiar quotations that may be hard to understand without some background information. The goal was to create a balanced collection that
- includes quotations that state a clear and direct message;
- presents a variety of opinions and viewpoints within each topic;
- reflects the knowledge and experiences of experts; for example, most of the quotes under Art are the words of great artists, and many of the quotes listed under Science and Technology come from scientists and inventors;
- combines the presentation of famous quotations drawn from English and American literature and history with lesser known, but equally powerful quotations that reflect the wisdom of diverse cultures and experiences.

Where Do These Quotations Come From?

The people whose words are included in this book are writers and leaders from many walks of life whose words have been published in some form. Novels, poems, plays, essays, and works of science, history, philosophy, and religion as well as interviews, magazine and newspaper articles, published diaries, letters, and speeches were reviewed to find these quotations. Other collections of quotations were also reviewed. Each quotation has been checked for accuracy.

Whenever possible, the names of people quoted are presented as they signed their names on their own work or by the simplest form of the name they are most often referred to by others. For example, the Englishman who served Queen Elizabeth I called himself Ralegh, not Raleigh.

A host of other choices also had to be made. What should be done when authoritative sources did not always agree on when a person was born or died or other basic facts about his or her life? What should be done when authoritative sources sometimes used different spellings for people's names? What should be done when different versions of the quotations, using slightly different wording, punctuation, or spelling, were found?

These choices were made by comparing the information set forth in the most highly respected reference books. When quotations come from transcripts of speeches, books that were first published a number of years ago, or works first said or written in languages other than English, there are often a variety of sources that present the information in slightly different manners. Care was taken to see which versions experts consider most accurate. For quotations that were first published in a language other than English, scholars were consulted whenever possible to help select translations that use simple language to present the true meaning of the original words.

The information in this book has been checked against the most recent editions of *Bartlett's Familiar Quotations, The Oxford Dictionary of Quotations, Merriam Webster's Biographical Dictionary, Compton's Encyclopedia*, and the *World Book Encyclopedia*. When these sources did not agree or provide sufficient information, additional research was done. Resources that proved to be especially helpful for this purpose were *My Soul Looks Back, 'Less I Forget: A Collection of Quotations by People of Color, The Whole World Book of Quotations, The New Quotable Woman, The Beacon Book of Quotations by Women, Current Biography*, and *The Encyclopedia of Religion*.

Even the most thorough reference books cannot specify with certainty when certain people were born or died. The following abbreviations are used to provide more information about dates and their accuracy:

A.D. and B.C. The most important thing to know about these appreviations is that Western historians have been using them for hundreds of years to indicate events that occurred before Christ (B.C.) and events that occured after his death (A.D.). For dates marked B.C., the higher the number gets, the longer ago the event occured. For dates marked A.D. (or not marked), the higher the number gets the more recent the date.

B. = born. This is used for people who are still alive or for whom only a birth date is known.

D. = died. This is used for people for whom only a date of death is known.

C. = *circa* (Latin for about).When C. appears before a date, the date is approximate, not certain.

FL. = *flourit* (Latin for flourished). FL. means that this date is even less certain than those marked as C.

In Their Own Words

Each quotation in this book was really said by the person identified, and reflects that person's general outlook on life and the topic. Because most quotations are taken from longer works, sometimes words appear in brackets [like this] to indicate a reference made earlier in what the person was saying. When ellipses . . . are used, some words have been left out. No words have been added or taken out that change the meaning of what the person really said.

Proverbs: Wisdom of the Ages

Some quotations can't be traced to a person, but instead are traced back to a culture. These old sayings are called proverbs. Proverbs are usually passed on through the spoken word, and sometimes different speakers use slightly different words to express the same proverb. Collections of proverbs, including *The Random House Dictionary of Popular Proverbs and Sayings* by Gregory Teitleman; *The Dictionary of American Proverbs* by Wolfgang Mieder, Stewart A. Kingsbury & Kelsie B. Harder; *The Prentice Hall Encyclopedia of World Proverbs* by Wolfgang Meider; and *Eyes That See Do Not Grow Old: The Proverbs of Mexico, Central America and South America* by Guy A. Zona, were among the works used to verify wording and origins of proverbs included in this book.

Who Said It First?

In some cases, a quotation might be attributed to one person in one source and to another person in another source. When this happens, it is often because both people are really quoting an old proverb or a line from an ancient source. In fact, some of the greatest writers in history, including Plutarch (who recorded the lives of great leaders of the ancient world) and Cervantes (who wrote *Don Quixote*), get credit for famous quotations that were probably common proverbs that everyone knew and used in everyday speech. They get credit for these words because they were the first to include them in a published work. Effort has been made to trace quotations back to their first published sources, or at least attribute them to the person who is best known for using the quotation.

ABILITY AND TALENT

Talent is like electricity—we do not understand electricity.
We use it.
MAYA ANGELOU (B. 1928)

Natural abilities are like natural plants
that need pruning by study.
FRANCIS BACON (1561–1626)

Behind every able man, there are always other able men.
CHINESE PROVERB

It is not enough to have a good mind.
The main thing is to use it well.
RENÉ DESCARTES (1596–1650)

Everyone must row with the oars he has.
ENGLISH PROVERB

The same man cannot be skilled in everything,
each has his special excellence.
EURIPIDES (C. 485–406 B.C.)

Sometimes it is more important to discover
what one cannot do than what one can do.
LIN YUTANG (1895–1976)

If I have made any valuable discoveries, it has been owing
more to patient attention than to any other talent.
ISAAC NEWTON (1642–1727)

Life is like a ten-speed bike. Most of us have gears we never use.
CHARLES SCHULZ (B. 1922)

They are able because they think they are able.
VIRGIL (70–19 B.C.)

ACHIEVEMENTS

By their fruits ye shall know them.
BIBLE: MATTHEW 7:20

One never sees what has been done.
One can only see what still needs to be done.
MARIE CURIE (1867–1934)

The reward of a thing well done is to have done it.
RALPH WALDO EMERSON (1803–1882)

Every race and every nation should be judged by
the best it has been able to produce, not by the worst.
JAMES WELDON JOHNSON (1871–1938)

When I read great literature, great drama, speeches or sermons,
I feel that the human mind has not achieved anything greater
than the ability to share feelings and thoughts through language.
JAMES EARL JONES (B. 1931)

Excellent things are rare.
PLATO (C. 428–348 B.C.)

ACTION

Actions speak louder than words.
AMERICAN PROVERB

The wheel that squeaks the loudest
is the one that gets the grease.
JOSH BILLINGS (1818–1885)

All great and honorable actions
are accompanied with great difficulties.
WILLIAM BRADFORD (1590–1657)

Human beings...must have action;
and they will make it if they cannot find it.
CHARLOTTE BRONTË (1816–1855)

The only thing necessary for the triumph of evil
is for good men to do nothing.
EDMUND BURKE (1729–1797)

Talk does not cook rice.
CHINESE PROVERB

Be always sure you're right—then go ahead.
DAVID CROCKETT (1786–1836)

Nothing is more terrible than ignorance in action.
JOHANN WOLFANG VON GOETHE (1749–1832)

The things that haven't been done before
Those are the things to try.
EDGAR GUEST (1881–1959)

I am only one,
But still I am one.
I cannot do everything,
But still I can do something;
And because I cannot do everything
I will not refuse to do the something that I can do.
EDWARD EVERETT HALL (1822–1909)

Seize the day, put no trust in tomorrow.
Carpe diem, quan minimum credula postero.
HORACE (65–8 B.C.)

Pray for the dead and fight for the living.
"MOTHER" JONES (1830–1930)

We judge ourselves by what we feel capable of doing,
while others judge us by what we have already done.
HENRY WADSWORTH LONGFELLOW (1807–1882)

Actions will be judged according to their intentions.
MUHAMMAD (C. 570–632)

The best time to do something is when it can be done.
WILLIAM PICKENS (1881–1954)

When you see a rattlesnake poised to strike,
you do not wait until he has struck before you crush him.
FRANKLIN D. ROOSEVELT (1882–1945)

Do not wait for leaders; do it alone, person to person.
MOTHER TERESA (1910–1997)

WAYS TO SAY: DON'T JUST TALK ABOUT IT, TAKE ACTION!

We have too many high-sounding words,
and too few actions that correspond to them.
ABIGAIL ADAMS (1744–1818)

A man of words and not of deeds
Is like a garden full of weeds.
MOTHER GOOSE

Words that do not match deeds are unimportant.
CHE GUEVARA (1928–1967)

Deeds are better things than words are,
Actions mightier than boastings.
HENRY WADSWORTH LONGFELLOW (1807–1882)

There is a great distance between said and done.
PUERTO RICAN PROVERB

Practice yourself what you preach.
TITUS MACCIUS PLAUTUS (C. 254–184 B.C.)

ADVICE

Be swift to hear, slow to speak, slow to wrath.
BIBLE: JAMES 1:19

My only advice is to stay awake, listen carefully,
and yell for help if you need it.
JUDY BLUME (B. 1938)

Listen and learn from people who have
already been where you want to go.
Benefit from their mistakes instead of repeating them.
BENJAMIN CARSON (B. 1957)

Nobody can give you wiser advice than yourself.
CICERO (106–43 B.C.)

When you have nothing to say, say nothing.
CHARLES CALEB COLTON (1780–1832)

When you have faults, do not fear to abandon them.
CONFUCIUS (551–479 B.C.)

The only good advice is a good example.
OSSIE DAVIS (B. 1917)

Life is short, and its up to you to make it sweet.
SADIE DELANY (B. 1889)

Whatever you are, be a good one.
ABRAHAM LINCOLN (1809–1865)

Learn to see, hear, and think for yourself.
MALCOLM X (1925–1965)

He who takes his own advice must suffer the consequences.
MEXICAN PROVERB

Do nothing you do not understand.
PYTHAGORAS (C. 582–500 B.C.)

Neither a borrower nor a lender be.
WILLIAM SHAKESPEARE (1564–1616)

It is better to keep your mouth shut and appear stupid
than to open it and remove all doubt.
MARK TWAIN (1835–1910)

BENJAMIN FRANKLIN AND POOR RICHARD'S ALMANAC

Few people have done as many different things as well as Ben Franklin. His community spirit helped create institutions such as the library and fire department in his home city, Philadelphia. His statesmanship helped craft the American Revolution and the political foundation for the new government created by the United States. He excelled as a scientist and inventor. Franklin also eagerly shared his opinions, and he was fond of offering advice to family and friends and, through his writing, to people he may have never met.

From 1729 to 1766, Franklin wrote and published *Poor Richard's Almanac.* Writing as Richard Saunders, he used wise and witty sayings to advise his readers. Each was selected by Franklin himself, but many had already been said or written by others. Franklin loved to read and found many of the sayings he used in his own library. Poor Richard's sayings made his almanac the most popular in its day, and many of his sayings, including the ones below, have survived through books like this one, to be shared again and again.

Early to bed and early to rise,
makes a man healthy, wealthy and wise.

In this world nothing can be said to be certain,
except death and taxes.

Time is money.

Never leave till tomorrow that which you can do today.

If you would not be forgotten,
As soon as you are dead and rotten,
Either write things worth reading,
Or do things worth the writing.

ANGER

It is easy to fly into a passion . . . but it is not easy to be angry with the right person, in the right way, and at the right time.
ARISTOTLE (384–322 B.C.)

A man that does not know how to be angry
does not know how to be good.
HENRY WARD BEECHER (1813–1887)

He that is slow to anger is better than the mighty;
and he that ruleth his spirit than he that taketh a city.
BIBLE: PROVERBS 16:32

Speak when you are angry, and you will make
the best speech you will ever regret.
AMBROSE BIERCE (1842–1914)

An angry man opens his mouth and shuts his eyes.
CATO THE ELDER (234–149 B.C.)

Anger is never without a reason, but seldom a good one.
BENJAMIN FRANKLIN (1706–1790)

Anger makes us all stupid.
JOHANNA SPYRI (1827–1901)

ANIMALS

I am fond of pigs. Dogs look up to us. Cats look down.
Pigs treat us as equals.
WINSTON CHURCHILL (1874–1965)

Bees are . . . Buccaneers of Buzz.
EMILY DICKINSON (1830–1886)

Nature's greatest masterpiece, an Elephant,
The only harmless great thing; the giant
Of beasts.
JOHN DONNE (1572–1631)

Animals are such agreeable friends—
they ask no questions, they pass no criticisms.
GEORGE ELIOT (1819–1880)

Wolves are brotherly. They love each other, and if you
learn to speak with them, they will love you, too.
JEAN CRAIGHEAD GEORGE (B. 1919)

When Allah created the horse, he said to the wind,
"I will create a creature to proceed thee."
MARGUERITE HENRY (1902–1997)

[Whales]...move like melting mountains.
X. J. KENNEDY (B. 1929)

Oh, a wonderous bird is the pelican!
His beak can hold more than his belican.
DIXON LANIER MERRITT (1879–1972)

Everyone wants to understand painting.
Why is there no attempt to understand the song of the birds?
PABLO PICASSO (1881–1973)

If we stop loving animals, aren't we
bound to stop loving humans, too?
ALEXANDER SOLZHENITSYN (B. 1918)

The bluebird carries the sky on its back.
HENRY DAVID THOREAU (1817–1862)

My favorite animal is the mule. . . . He knows when to stop eating—
and he knows when to stop working.
HARRY S TRUMAN (1884–1972)

I think I could turn and live with the animals, they are
so specific and self-contained, I could look at them long, long.
WALT WHITMAN (1819–1892)

The best thing about animals is that they do not talk much.
THORNTON WILDER (1897–1975)

AESOP SAID IT: THESE PROVERBS ARE REALLY ABOUT PEOPLE, NOT ANIMALS.

Aesop (FL. C. 550 B.C.) was a slave in ancient Greece who became famous for the stories he told. Each of his stories, or fables, teaches a lesson about how people should behave. Aesop often used animal characters who talked and acted like people in his stories. That is why some of the proverbs, including the ones below from his stories, seem to be about animals:

Beware of a wolf in sheep's clothing.
Meaning: Watch out for an enemy who pretends to be a friend.

Birds of a feather flock together.
*Meaning: People tend to stick with others with whom
they share common interests or belong to the same family.*

Every dog has its day.
Meaning: Every person will have some good luck and happiness.

Don't count your chickens before they are hatched.
*Meaning: Don't assume you will succeed before
a plan of activity is actually completed.*

DOGS

If you can't decide between a shepherd,
a setter or a poodle, get them all. . . . Adopt a mutt.
ASPCA SLOGAN

The dog was created especially for children.
He is the god of frolic.
HENRY WARD BEECHER (1813–1887)

A dog is man's best friend.
ENGLISH TRADITIONAL

CATS

Before a cat will condescend
To treat you like a trusted friend,
Some little token of esteem
Is needed, like a dish of cream.
T. S. ELIOT (1888–1965)

When I play with my cat—who knows? She may be amusing
herself with me more than I am with her.
MICHEL DE MONTAIGNE (1533–1592)

The trouble with a kitten is THAT
eventually, it becomes a CAT.
OGDEN NASH (1902–1971)

APOLOGIES AND EXCUSES

Any excuse will serve a tyrant.
AESOP (FL. C. 550 B.C.)

When the ape cannot reach the bananas he says they are sour.
BAMBARA PROVERB

This is the earliest I ever arrived late!
YOGI BERRA (B. 1925)

Ninety-nine percent of failures come from
people who have the habit of making excuses.
GEORGE WASHINGTON CARVER (C. 1864–1943)

Never make a defense or an apology before you are accused.
CHARLES I (1600–1649)

The bad workman always blames his tools.
CHINESE PROVERB

If you offend, ask for a pardon; if offended, forgive.
ETHIOPIAN PROVERB

He that is good at making excuses is seldom good at anything else.
BENJAMIN FRANKLIN (1706–1790)

Several excuses are always less convincing than one.
ALDOUS HUXLEY (1894–1963)

It takes less time to do a thing right
than to explain why you did it wrong.
HENRY WADSWORTH LONGFELLOW (1807–1882)

Excuse me for not answering your letter sooner.
I have been so busy not answering letters that I could not
get around to not answering yours in time.
GROUCHO MARX (1886–1961)

ART

Not everybody trusts paintings, but people believe photographs.
ANSEL ADAMS (1902–1984)

I don't know anything about art, but I know what I like.
GELETT BURGESS (1866–1951)

Armed with a paint-box, one cannot be bored.
WINSTON CHURCHILL (1874–1965)

Have no fear of perfection—you'll never reach it.
SALVADOR DALI (1904–1989)

Painting is very easy when you don't know how,
but very difficult when you do.
EDGAR DEGAS (1834–1917)

Every artist was first an amateur.
RALPH WALDO EMERSON (1803–1882)

Life is short, the art long.
HIPPOCRATES (c. 460–377 B.C.)

A man paints with his brains and not with his hands.
MICHELANGELO (1475–1564)

Nobody can count himself an artist unless
he carries a picture in his head before he paints it.
CLAUDE MONET (1840–1926)

To be an artist, one must . . . never shirk from the truth
as he understands it, never withdraw from life.
DIEGO RIVERA (1886–1957)

ARTISTS EXPLAIN THEIR OWN WORK

I take photographs because there are things that
nobody would see unless I photographed them.
DIANE ARBUS (1923–1971)

Brushes and paints are all I have
To speak the music of my soul.
GWENDOLYN BENNETT (1902–1981)

I paint myself because I am the subject I know best.
FRIDA KAHLO (1907–1954)

Pictures just come into my mind and I tell my heart to go ahead.
HORACE PIPPIN (1888–1946)

Every child is an artist. The problem is
how to remain an artist once [you] grow up.
PABLO PICASSO (1881–1973)

Less is more.
Meaning: The simplest way to do or say something is best.
(Well-known phrase popularized when this architect
explained the reasoning behind his creations.)
LUDWIG MIES VAN DER ROHE (1886–1969)

> When I begin painting I am in a state of
> unconsciousness; I suddenly forget that I am
> holding a brush in my hand.
> WU CHEN (1280–1354)

BEAUTY

Love is a great beautifier.
LOUISA MAY ALCOTT (1832–1888)

Beauty is power.
ARAB PROVERB

It is not at all necessary to be handsome or pretty;
all that is needed is charm.
SARAH BERNHARDT (1844–1923)

She walks in Beauty like the Night.
LORD BYRON (1788–1824)

Handsome is as handsome does.
GEOFFREY CHAUCER (C. 1343–1400)

Beauty is only skin deep.
ENGLISH TRADITIONAL

The night is beautiful;
So are the faces of my people.
LANGSTON HUGHES (1902–1967)

Beauty is in the eye of the beholder.
MARGARET WOLFE HUNGERFORD (1855–1897)

Beauty does not make the pot boil.
IRISH PROVERB

"Beauty is truth, truth beauty," that is all
Ye know on earth, and all ye need to know.
JOHN KEATS (1795–1821)

A thing of beauty is a joy forever.
JOHN KEATS (1795–1821)

It is because everyone recognizes beauty
that the idea of ugliness exists.
LAO-TZU (C. 604–C. 531 B.C.)

The Lord prefers common-looking people.
That is why he made so many of them.
ABRAHAM LINCOLN (1809–1865)

To any artist worthy of the name, all in nature is beautiful.
AUGUSTE RODIN (1840–1917)

Beauty too rich for use, for earth too dear.
(Romeo describing Juliet)
WILLIAM SHAKESPEARE (1564–1616)

Anyone who sees beauty and does not look at it will soon be poor.
YORUBA PROVERB

BEGINNINGS AND ENDINGS

Better is the end of a thing than the beginning thereof.
BIBLE: ECCLESIASTES 7:8

Nothing so difficult as a beginning . . . unless perhaps the end.
LORD BYRON (1788–1824)

"Begin at the beginning," the King said gravely, "and go on
till you come to the end; then stop."
LEWIS CARROLL (1832–1898)

It is far easier to start something than it is to finish it.
AMELIA EARHART (1898–1937)

All is well that ends well.
ENGLISH PROVERB

The value of any action lies in seeing it through to the end.
GENGHIS KHAN (C. 1162–1227)

Well begun is half done.
HORACE (65–8 B.C.)

A journey of a thousand miles begins with a single step.
LAO-TZU (C. 604–C. 531 B.C.)

Between the beginning and the end is always the middle.
MEXICAN PROVERB

You know that the beginning is the most important part of
any work, especially in the case of a young and tender thing:
for that is the time when the character is being formed.
PLATO (C. 428–348 B.C.)

BOOKS AND READING

Reading is to the mind what exercise is to the body.
JOSEPH ADDISON (1672–1719)

Some books are so familiar that reading them
is like being home again.
LOUISA MAY ALCOTT (1832–1888)

The answers you get from literature
depend upon the questions you pose.
MARGARET ATWOOD (B. 1939)

A classic is a book that has never finished saying what it has to say.
ITALO CALVINO (1923–1985)

A book is like a garden carried in a pocket.
CHINESE PROVERB

A truly great book should be read in youth,
again in maturity and once more in old age.
ROBERTSON DAVIES (1913–1995)

A book may be as great a thing as a battle.
BENJAMIN DISRAELI (1804–1881)

When you reread a classic you do not see more in the book than
you did before; you see more in *you* than there was before.
CLIFTON FADIMAN (B. 1904)

It is not true that we have only one life to live; if we can read,
we can live as many lives and as many kinds of lives as we wish.
S.I. HAYAKAWA (1906–1992)

I cannot live without books.
THOMAS JEFFERSON (1743–1826)

I have depended on books not only for pleasure and for
the wisdom they bring to all who read but also for that knowledge
which comes to others through their eyes and their ears.
HELEN KELLER (1880–1968)

My alma mater was books, a good library.
MALCOLM X (1925–1965)

Books are good enough in their own way,
but they are a mighty bloodless substitute for life.
ROBERT LOUIS STEVENSON (1850–1894)

When I am reading a book, whether wise or silly,
it seems to be alive and talking to me.
JONATHAN SWIFT (1667–1745)

The man who does not read good books
has no advantage over the man who cannot read them.
MARK TWAIN (1835–1910)

CHANGE

I change myself, I change the world.
GLORIA ANZALDÚA (B. 1942)

The man who never alters his opinion is like
standing water, and breeds reptiles of the mind.
WILLIAM BLAKE (1757–1827)

When you have faults, do not fear to abandon them.
CONFUCIUS (551–479 B.C.)

I thought I could change the world. It took me a hundred years to
figure out I can't change the world. I can only change Bessie.
BESSIE DELANY (1891–1995)

A foolish consistency is the hobgoblin of little minds.
*Meaning: Only rigid, narrow-minded people refuse to change
or accept new ideas and new ways of doing things.*
RALPH WALDO EMERSON (1803–1882)

Everything changes but change itself. Everything flows and nothing
remains the same. . . . You cannot step twice into the same river,
for other waters and yet others go flowing ever on.
HERACLITUS (C. 540–C. 480 B.C.)

There is a certain relief in change, even though it be from bad to worse; as I have often found in traveling in a stagecoach that it is often a comfort to shift one's position and be bruised in a new place.
WASHINGTON IRVING (1783–1859)

The more things change, the more they remain the same.
ALPHONSE KARR (1808–1890)

New opinions are always suspected, and usually opposed, without any other reason but because they are not already common.
JOHN LOCKE (1632–1704)

Never doubt that a small group of thoughtful, committed citizens can change the world. Indeed, it's the only thing that ever has.
MARGARET MEAD (1901–1978)

Each change brings a little good, each change brings a little bad.
MEXICAN PROVERB

Back when dinosaurs ruled the earth. . . .Women made the coffee and men made the decisions. No more. We have changed that.
ANN RICHARDS (B. 1933)

All big changes in human history have been arrived at slowly and through many compromises.
ELEANOR ROOSEVELT (1884–1962)

He who cannot change the very fabric of his thought will never. . . make any progress.
ANWAR al–SADAT (1918–1981)

Modern inventions have banished the spinning wheel,
and the same law of progress makes the woman of today
a different woman from her grandmother.
ELIZABETH CADY STANTON (1815–1902)

If you want to make enemies, try and change something.
WOODROW WILSON (1856–1924)

CHARACTER

It is not in the still calm of life . . . that great characters
are formed. . . . Great neccessities call out great virtues.
ABIGAIL ADAMS (1744–1818)

Fame is vapor, popularity an accident, riches take wing.
Only one thing endures and that is character.
JOSEPH ADDISON (1672–1719)

A good name is rather to be chosen than great riches.
BIBLE: PROVERBS 22:1

Distance tests a horse's strength. Time reveals a person's character.
CHINESE PROVERB

The man who fights for his fellow-man
is a better man than one who fights for himself.
CLARENCE DARROW (1857–1938)

It is not what you call us, but what we answer that matters.
DJUKA PROVERB

Parents can only give good advice or put them on the right paths,
but the final forming of a person's character lies in their own hands.
ANNE FRANK (1929–1945)

A man shows his character by what he laughs at.
GERMAN PROVERB

A man's character is his fate.
HERACLITUS (C. 540–480 B.C.)

A good head and a good heart are always a formidable combination.
NELSON MANDELA (B. 1918)

I think that there is only one quality worse than
hardness of the heart, and that is softness of the head.
THEODORE ROOSEVELT (1858–1919)

We write our own destiny. We become what we do.
SOONG MEI-LING (MADAME CHIANG KAI-SHEK) (1901–1987)

The best index to a person's character is
(a) how he treats people who can't do him any good,
(b) how he treats people who cannot fight back.
ABIGAIL VAN BUREN ("DEAR ABBY") (B. 1918)

Character, not circumstances, make the man.
BOOKER T. WASHINGTON (1856–1915)

It is better to be alone than in bad company.
GEORGE WASHINGTON (1732–1799)

CHOICES

No man can serve two masters.
BIBLE: MATTHEW 6:24

I would rather be right than be President.
HENRY CLAY (1777–1852)

The die is cast.
Meaning: The choice is made.
JULIUS CAESAR (100–44 B.C.)

Two roads diverged in a wood, and I—
I took the one less traveled by,
And that has made all the difference.
(from "The Road Not Taken")
ROBERT FROST (1874–1963)

It is the ability to choose which makes us human.
MADELINE L'ENGLE (B. 1918)

If your head tells you one thing and your heart
tells you another, before you do anything, you should first decide
whether you have a better head or a better heart.
MARILYN VOS SAVANT (B. 1946)

You have brains in your head.
You have feet in your shoes.
You can steer yourself
Any direction you choose.
(*from* Oh, the Places You'll Go!*)*
DR. SEUSS (1904–1991)

There's small choice in rotten apples.
WILLIAM SHAKESPEARE (1564–1616)

CITIZENSHIP AND PATRIOTISM

Civilization is a method of living,
an attitude of equal respect for all men.
JANE ADDAMS (1860–1935)

We will work to increase the public's sense of duty
to our City. In all ways, we will leave this city
for the next generation—not only not less, but greater
and more beautiful than it was when it was given to us.
(*oath taken at age 17 by young men of the city-state*)
ATHENIAN OATH (C. 450 B.C.)

If I should die think only this of me:
That there's some corner of a foreign field
That is forever England.
RUPERT BROOKE (1887–1915)

There is nothing wrong with America
that cannot be cured by what is right with America.
WILLIAM CLINTON (B. 1946)

Patriotism means looking out for yourself
by looking out for your country.
CALVIN COOLIDGE (1872–1933)

Our country! In her intercourse with foreign nations
may she always be in the right; but our country, right or wrong.
STEPHEN DECATUR (1779–1820)

The meaning of America is the possibilities of the common man.
W.E.B. DU BOIS (1868–1963)

Let him who loves his country in his heart,
and not with his lips only follow me.
GIUSEPPE GARIBALDI (1807–1882)

I only regret that I have but one life to lose for my country.
NATHAN HALE (1755–1776)

What has made this nation great? Not its heroes but its households.
SARAH JOSEPHA HALE (1788–1879)

I try to do something for my country because I live here.
VÁCLAV HAVEL (B. 1936)

I am not a Virginian, but an American.
PATRICK HENRY (1736–1799)

I, for one, know of no sweeter sight
for a man's eyes than his own country.
HOMER (C. 700 B.C.)

America is like a quilt [made of] many patches,
many pieces, many colors, many sizes, all woven
and held together by a common thread.
JESSE JACKSON (B. 1941)

And so, my fellow Americans, ask not what your country
can do for you, ask what you can do for your country.
My fellow citizens of the world, ask not what America will do
for you, but what together we can do for the freedom of man.
(Inaugural address, Jan. 20, 1961)
JOHN F. KENNEDY (1917–1963)

National honor is national property of the highest value.
JAMES MONROE (1758–1831)

Breathes there the man, with soul so dead,
Who never to himself hath said,
This is my own, my native land!
SIR WALTER SCOTT (1771–1832)

I am not an Athenian or a Greek, but a citizen of the world.
SOCRATES (469–399 B.C.)

Canada is not a country for the cold of heart or the cold of feet.
PIERRE ELLIOTT TRUDEAU (B. 1919)

COMMUNITY AND CITY LIFE

A city is in many respects a great business corporation,
but in other respects it is enlarged housekeeping.
JANE ADDAMS (1860–1935)

A library should be the heart of a city. With its storehouse of
knowledge, it liberates, informs, teaches, and enthralls.
RUDOLFO ANAYA (B. 1937)

It takes a village to raise a child.
Meaning: Everyone in a community, not just a child's parents,
must help the child learn and grow.
(BENIN PROVERB POPULARIZED IN THE UNITED STATES WHEN
FIRST LADY HILLARY RODHAM CLINTON USED IT AS THE SOURCE
FOR A TITLE AND THEME OF A BOOK SHE WROTE.)

Thou shalt love thy neighbor as thyself.
BIBLE: LEVITICUS 19:18

A city that is set on a hill cannot be hid.
BIBLE: MATTHEW 5:14

We make our friends; we make our enemies;
but God sends us our neighbors.
LORD G.K. CHESTERTON (1874–1936)

No man is an island entire of itself . . . every man is a
piece of the continent, a part of the main . . . any man's death
diminishes me, because I am involved in mankind.
JOHN DONNE (1572–1631)

Service is the rent we pay for living. It is the very purpose
of life and not something you do in your spare time.
MARIAN WRIGHT EDELMAN (B. 1939)

A sufficient measure of civilization is the influence of good women.
RALPH WALDO EMERSON (1803–1882)

Good fences make good neighbors.
(New England proverb popularized by Frost in his poem "Mending Wall.")
ROBERT FROST (1874–1963)

If farmers do not work their fields,
the people in the town will die of hunger.
GUINEAN PROVERB

In all ways and at all times [people] have a need
for sharing life with others and the search for community.
VIRGINIA HAMILTON (B. 1936)

When a man is tired of London, he is tired of life;
for there is in London all that life can afford.
SAMUEL JOHNSON (1709–1784)

What is not good for the swarm is not good for the bee.
MARCUS AURELIUS (A.D. 121–180)

The new electronic interdependence recreates
the world in the image of a global village.
MARSHALL MCCLUHAN (1911– 1980)

The greatest city is that which
has the greatest men and women in it.
If it be a few ragged huts it is still
the greatest city in the whole world.
WALT WHITMAN (1819–1892)

If each person sweeps in front of his or her own door,
the whole street is clean.
YIDDISH PROVERB

COMPLIMENTS AND INSULTS

He could fiddle all the bugs off a sweet-potato vine.
STEPHEN VINCENT BENÉT (1898–1943)

He who praises everybody, praises nobody.
JAMES BOSWELL (1740–1795)

Imitation is the sincerest of flattery.
(often misquoted as "form of flattery")
CHARLES CALEB COLTON (1780–1832)

Tart words make no friends. A spoonful of honey
will catch more flies than a gallon of vinegar.
BENJAMIN FRANKLIN (1706–1790)

[He is] a very modest man.
But then he has much to be modest about.
WINSTON CHURCHILL (1874–1965)

He that flings dirt at another dirties himself most.
THOMAS FULLER (1608–1661)

Sir, you have but two topics, yourself and me. I am sick of both.
SAMUEL JOHNSON (1709–1784)

If you speak insults you shall also hear them.
LATIN PROVERB

It is as great an error to speak well of an unworthy man
as it is to speak ill of a good man.
LEONARDO DA VINCI (1452–1519)

I never forget a face, but I'll make an exception in your case.
GROUCHO MARX (1895–1977)

He never said a foolish thing,
Nor ever did a wise one.
epitaph for King Charles II
JOHN WILMOT, EARL OF ROCHESTER (1647–1680)

No matter how you slice it, it's still baloney.
ALFRED SMITH (1873–1944)

CONFIDENCE

If you think you can, you can.
And if you think you can't, you are right.
AMERICAN TRADITIONAL

Confidence adds more to the conversation than cleverness.
FRENCH PROVERB

If you have no confidence in [yourself] you are
twice defeated in the race of life. With confidence,
you have won even before you have started.
MARCUS GARVEY (1887–1940)

BOASTS AND BRAGS

Had I been present at the creation, I would have given
some useful hints for the better ordering of the universe.
ALFONSO X (1221–1284)

I came, I saw, I conquered.
JULIUS CAESAR (100–44 B.C.)

I'm . . . half horse, half alligator, a little touched with
the snapping turtle; can wade the Mississippi,
leap the Ohio, ride upon a streak of lightning. . . .
[I] can whip my weight in wildcats.
DAVID CROCKETT (1786–1836)

It ain't braggin' if you can do it.
DIZZY DEAN (1911–1974)

What an artist dies in me.
NERO (37–68 A.D.)

COOPERATION AND UNITY

Great discoveries and improvements . . .
involve the cooperation of many minds.
ALEXANDER GRAHAM BELL (1847–1922)

Whither thou goest, I will go; and where thou lodgest, I will lodge:
thy people shall be my people, and thy God my God.
BIBLE: THE BOOK OF RUTH 1:16

If a house be divided against itself, that house cannot stand.
BIBLE: MARK 3:25

All for one, one for all, that is our motto.
ALEXANDRE DUMAS (1802–1870)

When spiderwebs unite they can tie up a lion.
ETHIOPIAN PROVERB

We must indeed all hang together,
or assuredly we shall all hang separately.
(said upon signing the Declaration of Independence)
BENJAMIN FRANKLIN (1706–1790)

Let us be like the lines that lead to the center of a circle,
uniting there and not like parallel lines that never join.
HASIDIC PROVERB

We must live together as brothers or perish together as fools.
MARTIN LUTHER KING, JR. (1929–1968)

I have seen that in any great undertaking it is not enough
for a man to depend simply upon himself.
LONE MAN (ISNA LA-WICA) (C. LATE 19TH CENTURY)

i have noticed
that when
chickens quit
quarreling over their
food they often find that there is
enough for all of them
i wonder if
it might not
be the same way
with the
human race
DON MARQUIS (1878–1937)

Africans believe in . . . *ubunutu botho.* It means the
essence of being human. . . . It recognizes that my humanity
is bound up in yours, for we can only be human together.
DESMOND TUTU (B. 1931)

Liberty *and* Union, now and forever, one and inseparable.
DANIEL WEBSTER (1782–1852)

COURAGE

It is easy to be brave from a distance.
AESOP (FL. C. 550 B.C.)

Tell a man he is brave and you help him become so.
THOMAS CARLYLE (1795–1881)

He who has courage and faith will never perish in misery!
ANNE FRANK (1929–1945)

Heroes are made in the hour of defeat.
MOHANDAS GANDHI (1869–1948)

[What is the definition of "guts"?] Grace under pressure.
ERNEST HEMINGWAY (1899–1961)

One man with courage makes a majority.
ANDREW JACKSON (1767–1845)

It's better to be a lion for a day than a sheep all your life.
SISTER ELIZABETH KENNY (1880–1952)

Whoever can see through all fear
Will always be safe.
LAO-TZU (C. 604–531 B.C.)

Courage is the ladder on which all other virtues mount.
CLAIRE BOOTHE LUCE (1903–1987)

A noble, courageous man shows patience in adversity.
PACHACUTEC INCA YUPANQUI (1438–1471)

Courage is doing what you're afraid to do.
There can be no courage unless you're scared.
EDDIE RICKENBACKER (1890–1973)

You gain strength, courage and confidence by every
experience in which you stop to look fear directly in the face.
ELEANOR ROOSEVELT (1884–1962)

We have nothing to fear but fear itself.
FRANKLIN D. ROOSEVELT (1882–1945)

One must think like a hero to
behave like a merely decent human being.
MAY SARTON (1912–1995)

CREATIVITY AND IDEAS

A man who has no imagination has no wings.
MUHAMMAD ALI (B. 1942)

I can't understand why people are frightened of new ideas.
I'm frightened of the old ones.
JOHN CAGE (1912–1992)

The only way of discovering the limits of the possible
is to venture a little past them into the impossible.
ARTHUR C. CLARKE (B. 1917)

I think therefore, I am.
Cogito ergo sum.
RENÉ DESCARTES (1596–1650)

The Brain—is wider than the Sky.
EMILY DICKINSON (1830–1886)

Imagination is more important than knowledge.
ALBERT EINSTEIN (1879–1955)

You can kill a man, but you can't kill an idea.
MEDGAR EVERS (1926–1963)

Thinking is the hardest work there is,
which is the probable reason why so few engage in it.
HENRY FORD (1863–1947)

All intelligent thoughts have already been thought;
what is necessary is only to try to think them again.
JOHANN WOLFANG VON GOETHE (1749–1832)

Never be afraid to sit awhile and think.
LORRAINE HANSBERRY (1930–1965)

A man is not idle because he is absorbed in thought.
There is a visible labor and there is an invisible labor.
VICTOR HUGO (1802–1885)

A man may die, nations rise and fall, but an idea lives on.
JOHN F. KENNEDY (1917–1963)

If you are possessed with an idea, you'll find it
expressed everywhere, you'll even *smell* it.
THOMAS MANN (1875–1955)

Errors and exaggerations do not matter.
What matters is boldness in thinking.
JOSÉ CLEMENTE OROZCO (1883–1949)

An artist's style is . . . a continuous process of invention.
OCTAVIO PAZ (B. 1914)

New ideas are one of the most overrated concepts of our time.
Most of the important ideas that we live with aren't new at all.
ANDY ROONEY (B. 1919)

The brain is like a muscle.
When it is in use we feel very good.
Understanding is joyous.
CARL SAGAN (1934–1996)

Vision is the art of seeing things invisible.
JONATHAN SWIFT (1667–1745)

SOCRATES: A MAN OF IDEAS

Like many of the great philosphers of the ancient world, Socrates (469–399 B.C.) explored ideas on any and every subject. Socrates believed that if people thought things through, they could discover the correct way to act in any situation. Socrates shared his ideas in the streets, marketplaces, and schools of ancient Athens. He taught by questioning his students and pointing out flaws in their answers. The rulers of Athens heard that Socrates was teaching his pupils to question their right to rule and decided to put a stop to Socrates's ideas by sentencing him to death. Socrates accepted his sentence and drank a cup of poison, saying "I was really too honest a human to be a politician and live."

Although Socrates was considered one of the most learned people of his day, he never wrote down his teachings. Some historians believe Socrates could neither read nor write, possibly due to a learning disability. However, his words survive through the writings of his most dedicated pupil, Plato, as well as the works of the historians Xenophon and Plutarch and the playwright Aristophanes, who often poked fun at Socrates in his plays.

My plainness of speech makes them hate me,
and what is their hatred but a proof that I am speaking the truth?

I know nothing except the fact of my ignorance.

Let him who would move the world first move himself.

The unexamined life is not worth living.

CURIOSITY

Curiosity killed the cat.
AMERICAN PROVERB

I wanted to know the name of every stone and flower and insect
and bird and beast . . . but there was no one to tell me.
GEORGE WASHINGTON CARVER (C. 1864–1943)

Be less curious about people and more curious about ideas.
MARIE CURIE (1867–1934)

Research is formalized curiosity.
It is poking and prying with a purpose.
ZORA NEALE HURSTON (C. 1901–1960)

Curiosity is one of the permanent and certain
characteristics of a vigorous mind.
SAMUEL JOHNSON (1709–1784)

He that breaks a thing to find out what it is
has left the path of wisdom.
J.R.R. TOLKIEN (1892–1973)

DANCE

Dancing is a sweat job. . . . It takes time
to get a dance right to create something memorable.
FRED ASTAIRE (1899–1987)

Someone once said to me that dancers work as hard as policemen:
always alert, always tense. But you see, policemen
don't have to be beautiful at the same time!
GEORGE BALANCHINE (1904–1983)

Whether it's dancing or living, learn by practice.
MARTHA GRAHAM (1894–1991)

People come to see beauty, and I dance to give it to them.
JUDITH JAMISON (B. 1944)

To sing well and to dance well is to be well educated.
PLATO (C. 428–348 B.C.)

I see the dance being used as a means of communication—
to express what is too deep, too fine for words.
RUTH ST. DENIS (1879–1968)

DEMOCRACY

No one pretends that democracy is perfect or all-wise.
Indeed, it has been said that democracy is the
worst form of government except all those other forms
that have been tried from time to time.
WINSTON CHURCHILL (1874–1965)

As I would not be a *slave*, so I would not be a *master*.
This expresses my idea of democracy. Whatever differs from this,
to the extent of the difference, is no democracy.
ABRAHAM LINCOLN (1809–1865)

To defend democracy is to defend the possibility of change.
In turn, change alone can strengthen democracy.
OCTAVIO PAZ (B. 1914)

A community is democratic only when the humblest
and weakest person can enjoy the highest civil, economic, and
social rights that the biggest and the most powerful possess.
A. PHILIP RANDOLPH (1889–1979)

Democracy is not a fragile flower but it still needs cultivating.
RONALD REAGAN (B. 1911)

Democracy is the recurrent suspicion that more than half
of the people are right more than half of the time.
E. B. WHITE (1899–1985)

DREAMS AND GOALS

If you don't know where you want to go,
any road will take you there.
AFRICAN-AMERICAN PROVERB

Ah, but a man's reach should exceed his grasp,
Or what's a heaven for?
ROBERT BROWNING (1812–1889)

Personal motto: Honesty, industry, concentration.
ANDREW CARNEGIE (1835–1919)

A dream is a wish your heart makes.
WALT DISNEY (1901–1966)

Before taking steps the wise man knows
the object and end of his journey.
W.E.B. Du Bois (1868–1963)

Resolved, never to do anything which I should be
afraid to do if it were the last hour of my life.
Jonathan Edwards (1703–1758)

Hitch your wagon to a star.
Ralph Waldo Emerson (1803–1882)

Hold fast to dreams
For if dreams die
Life is a broken-winged bird
That cannot fly.
Langston Hughes (1902–1967)

Every man has his peculiar ambition.
Abraham Lincoln (1809–1865)

Nothing happens unless first a dream.
Carl Sandburg (1878–1967)

You see things; and you say, "Why?"
But I dream things that never were; and I say, "Why not?"
George Bernard Shaw (1856–1950)

My dreams were all my own;
I accounted for them to nobody. They were my refuge
when annoyed—my dearest pleasure when free.
MARY SHELLEY (1797–1851)

I dream my painting, and then I paint my dream.
VINCENT VAN GOGH (1853–1890)

"I HAVE A DREAM": MARTIN LUTHER KING, JR.

Martin Luther King, Jr., (1929–1968) is probably the most often quoted American of his time. On August 28, 1963, Dr. King spoke on the mall in Washington, D.C. In his speech Dr. King told his audience that he had a dream, a dream of an America in which all races coexisted in harmony and enjoyed equal rights and privileges, an America where all people would rejoice because they were "free at last."

More than 250,000 people stood between the Lincoln Memorial and the Washington Memorial and listened to Dr. King's words. Millions more heard his words on the radio and on television. Many people who heard Dr. King that day came to share his dream and realize that the time was right for change. A few months after Dr. King gave this speech, the U.S. government passed a new Civil Rights Act, and in October, 1964, Dr. King received the Nobel Peace Prize for his efforts to bring about peaceful change. The following quotes show how he was able to say a great deal in very few words.

I have a dream that my four little children will one day
live in a nation where they will not be judged by the color of
their skin, but by the content of their character.

The old law of an eye for an eye leaves everybody blind.

Injustice anywhere is a threat to justice everywhere.

We may all have come on different ships,
but we're in the same boat now.

EDUCATION AND LEARNING

Learning is not attained by chance, it must be
sought for with ardor and attended to with diligence.
ABIGAIL ADAMS (1744–1818)

What sculpture is to a block of marble,
education is to the human soul.
JOSEPH ADDISON (1672–1719)

The fate of empires depends on the education of youth.
ARISTOTLE (384–322 B.C.)

Knowledge itself is power.
FRANCIS BACON (1561–1626)

It ain't what a man don't know that makes him a fool,
but what he does know that ain't so.
JOSH BILLINGS (1818–1885)

It is a greater work to educate a child . . . than to rule a state.
WILLIAM ELLERY CHANNING (1780–1842)

A little learning, indeed may be a dangerous thing,
but the want of learning is a calamity to any people.
FREDERICK DOUGLASS (C. 1818–1895)

Fear always springs from ignorance.
RALPH WALDO EMERSON (1803–1882)

Learning makes a man fit company for himself.
THOMAS FULLER (1654–1734)

Knowledge is of two kinds. We know a subject ourselves,
or we know where we can find information upon it.
SAMUEL JOHNSON (1709–1784)

Education, then, beyond all other devices of human origin,
is a great equalizer of the conditions of men.
HORACE MANN (1796–1859)

The pupil who is never required to do what he cannot do,
never does what he can do.
JOHN STUART MILL (1806–1873)

Seek knowledge from the cradle to the grave.
MUHAMMAD (570–632)

Learning is the best of all wealth. It is easy to carry.
Thieves cannot steal it. Neither fire nor water can destroy it,
and far from decreasing, it increases with giving.
NĀLĀDIYAR-DIVYA

'Tis education forms the common mind:
Just as the twig is bent, the tree's inclin'd.
ALEXANDER POPE (1688–1744)

A little learning is a dang'rous thing.
ALEXANDER POPE (1688–1744)

You can get help from teachers, but you are going to have to
learn a lot by yourself, sitting alone in a room.
DR. SEUSS (1909–1991)

A mind is a terrible thing to waste.
UNITED NEGRO COLLEGE FUND SLOGAN (C. 1980)

Not to know is bad. Not to wish to know is worse.
WOLOF WEST AFRICAN PROVERB

Education is not the filling of a pail but the lighting of a fire.
WILLIAM BUTLER YEATS (1865–1939)

TEACHERS ON TEACHING

Teaching is not a lost art, but the regard for it is a lost tradition.
JACQUES BARZUN (B. 1907)

The good teacher makes the poor student good
and the good student superior. When our students fail,
we as teachers, too, have failed.
MARVA COLLINS (B. 1936)

In the pursuit of knowledge, every day something is added.
LAO-TZU (C. 604–531 B.C.)

A professor can never better distinguish himself in his work
than by encouraging a clever pupil.
CAROLUS LINNAEUS (CARL VON LINNÉ) (1707–1778)

I touch the future. I teach.
CHRISTA McAULIFFE (1948–1986)

To teach is to learn twice over.
JOSEPH JOUBERT (1754–1824)

My joy in learning is partly that it enables me to teach.
LUCIUS ANNAEUS SENECA (C. 4 B.C.–A.D. 65)

My heart is singing for joy...The light of
understanding has shone in my little pupil's mind,
and behold, all things are changed.
ANNE SULLIVAN (1866–1936)

If you can read this, thank a teacher.
U.S. BUMPER STICKER

EFFORT AND ENTHUSIASM

Slow and steady wins the race.
AESOP (FL. C. 550 B.C.)

When pain ends, gain ends too.
ROBERT BROWNING (1812–1889)

Never give in, never give in, never, never, never, never—
in nothing great or small, large or petty—never give in
except to convictions of honor and good sense.
WINSTON CHURCHILL (1874–1965)

If there is no struggle there is no progress.
FREDERICK DOUGLASS (1817–1895)

Genius is one percent inspiration
and ninety-nine percent perspiration.
THOMAS EDISON (1847–1931)

Nothing great was ever achieved without enthusiasm.
RALPH WALDO EMERSON (1803–1882)

Leave no stone unturned.
Meaning: Keep looking until you find what you are looking for.
EURIPIDES (C. 485–406 B.C.)

No person who is enthusiastic about his work
has anything to fear from life.
SAMUEL GOLDWYN (1882–1974)

Life is something like a trumpet.
If you don't put anything into it, you don't get anything out.
W. C. HANDY (1873–1958)

Trifles make perfection, but perfection is no trifle.
ITALIAN PROVERB

I think the one lesson that I have learned
is that there is no substitute for paying attention.
DIANE SAWYER (B. 1946)

My candle burns at both ends;
It will not last the night;
But, ah, my foes, and, oh, my friends—
It gives a lovely light.
EDNA ST. VINCENT MILLAY (1892–1950)

You can't cross the sea
merely by standing and staring at the water.
RABINDRANATH TAGORE (1861–1941)

The difficult is done at once; the impossible takes a little longer.
ANTHONY TROLLOPE (1815–1882)

Keep trying and see what fate brings.
VIETNAMESE PROVERB

ENVY AND JEALOUSY

The grass is always greener on the other side of the fence.
AMERICAN PROVERB

Compete. Don't envy.
ARAB PROVERB

Thou shalt not covet thy neighbor's house . . .
nor any thing that is thy neighbor's.
BIBLE: EXODUS 20:12–17

It is better to be envied than pitied.
HERODOTUS (C. 485–C. 425 B.C.)

Achieve excellence yourself in some way.
Then you will not sorrow when you see excellence in others.
RUMI (1207–1273)

O, beware, my lord, of jealousy!
It is the green-eyed monster which doth mock
The meat it feeds on.
WILLIAM SHAKESPEARE (1564–1616)

Envy is a worm that gnaws at the innards of ambitious men.
PACHACUTEC INCA YUPANQUI (1438–1471)

EXCEPTIONS

There is an exception to every rule.
RUSSIAN PROVERB

EXPERIENCE

There are some things you learn best in calm, and some in storm.
WILLA CATHER (1873–1947)

I hear and I forget. I see and I remember.
I do and I understand.
CHINESE PROVERB

If everything could be done twice,
everything would be done better.
COSTA RICAN PROVERB

Mistakes are a fact of life.
It is the response to error that counts.
NIKKI GIOVANNI (B. 1943)

I have but one lamp by which my feet are guided,
and that is the lamp of experience.
PATRICK HENRY (1736–1799)

Experience is not what happens to a man.
It is what a man does with what happens to him.
ALDOUS HUXLEY (1894–1963)

Experience is a hard school, but a fool will learn in no other.
IRISH PROVERB

A proverb is no proverb to you till life has illustrated it.
JOHN KEATS (1795–1821)

Experience is the best teacher.
LATIN PROVERB

Where I was born and where and how I lived is unimportant. It is
what I have done with where I have been that should be of interest.
GEORGIA O'KEEFE (1887–1986)

The person who has lived the most is not the one who has
lived the longest, but the one with the richest experiences.
JEAN JACQUES ROUSSEAU (1712–1778)

Experience is the name everyone gives to their mistakes.
SIR WALTER SCOTT (1771–1832)

Be careful to get out of experience all the wisdom
that is in it—not like the cat that sits down on the hot stove.
She will never sit down on the hot stove lid again—
but she also will never sit down on a cold one anymore.
MARK TWAIN (1835–1910)

FAITH AND HOPE

He who has help has hope, and he who has hope has everything.
ARAB PROVERB

Hope is a good breakfast, but it is a bad supper.
FRANCIS BACON (1561–1626)

We shall overcome, we shall overcome, someday.
BAPTIST HYMN

When it is dark enough, you can see the stars.
CHARLES A. BEARD (1874–1948)

Without faith, nothing is possible.
With it, nothing is impossible.
MARY MCLEOD BETHUNE (1875–1955)

Man doth not live by bread only.
BIBLE: DEUTERONOMY 8:3

Faith is the substance of things hoped for,
the evidence of things not seen.
BIBLE: HEBREWS 11:1

The kingdom of God is within you.
BIBLE: MARK 17:21

The Lord is my shepherd; I shall not want.
BIBLE: PSALMS 23:1

While there's life, there's hope.
MARCUS TULLIUS CICERO (106–43 B.C.)

God moves in a mysterious way.
WILLIAM COWPER (1731–1800)

"Hope" is the thing with feathers—
That perches in the soul—
And sings the tune without the words—
And never stops—at all—
EMILY DICKINSON (1830–1886)

He that lives upon hope will die fasting.
BENJAMIN FRANKLIN (1706–1790)

It is always darkest before the dawn.
THOMAS FULLER (1654–1734)

Everything on the earth has a purpose,
every disease an herb to cure it,
and every person a mission.
MOURNING DOVE (CHRISTINE QUINTASKET) (1888–1936)

Hope for the best and prepare for the worst.
THOMAS NORTON (1532–84)

He who does not hope to win has already lost.
JOSÉ JOAQUIN DE OLMEDO (1780–1847)

Hope springs eternal in the human breast:
Man never is, but always to be blest.
ALEXANDER POPE (1688–1744)

FAMILY

What strange creatures brothers are!
JANE AUSTIN (1775–1817)

Honor thy father and thy mother.
BIBLE: EXODUS 20:12

It's a funny thing about mothers and fathers.
Even when their own child is the most disgusting blister you could
ever imagine, they still think that he or she is wonderful.
ROALD DAHL (1916–1990)

Blood is thicker than water.
Meaning: Relationships and loyalty
to family members are stronger than with others.
ENGLISH PROVERB (FIRST WRITTEN DOWN
BY JOHN LYDGATE IN 1412)

A mother is not a person to lean on
but a person to make leaning unnecessary.
DOROTHY CANFIELD FISHER (1879–1958)

Grandparents somehow sprinkle
a sense of stardust over grandchildren.
ALEX HALEY (1921–1992)

Your children need your presence more than your presents.
JESSE JACKSON (B. 1941)

Love is the chain whereby to bind a child to his parents.
ABRAHAM LINCOLN (1809–1865)

In the baby lies the future of the world. . . . His father
must take him to the highest hill to see what his world is like.
MAYAN PROVERB

He who does not honor his wife dishonors himself.
MEXICAN PROVERB

For there is no friend like a sister
In calm or stormy weather. . . .
CHRISTINA ROSSETTI (1830–1894)

Big sisters are the crab grass on the lawn of life.
(Linus describing Lucy)
CHARLES SCHULZ (B. 1922)

How sharper than a serpent's tooth it is
To have a thankless child!
WILLIAM SHAKESPEARE (1564–1616)

A brother is like one's shoulder.
SOMALIAN PROVERB

Motherhood is the most important of all professions—requiring
more knowledge than any other department in human affairs.
ELIZABETH CADY STANTON (1815–1902)

Happy families are all alike;
every unhappy family is unhappy in its own way.
LEO TOLSTOY (1828–1910)

The hand that rocks the cradle
Is the hand that rules the world.
WILLIAM ROSS WALLACE (1819–1881)

God could not be everywhere, and therefore he made mothers.
YIDDISH SAYING

FOOD

The way to a man's heart is through his stomach.
JOHN ADAMS (1735–1826)

You are what you eat.
AMERICAN SAYING

A man has no better thing under the sun,
than to eat, and to drink, and to be merry.
BIBLE: ECCLESIASTES 8:15

Never work before breakfast;
if you have to work before breakfast, eat your breakfast first.
JOSH BILLINGS (1818–1885)

An army marches on its stomach.
NAPOLEON I (NAPOLEON BONAPARTE) (1769–1821)

Research tells us that fourteen out of any ten people like chocolate.
SANDRA BOYNTON (B. 1953)

Tell me what you eat, and I shall tell you what you are.
ANTHELME BRILLAT-SAVARIN (1755–1826)

I doubt whether the world holds for any one a more
soul-stirring surprise than the first adventure with ice cream.
HEYWOOD HALE BROUN (1888–1939)

Watermelon—it's a good fruit.
You eat, you drink, you wash your face.
ENRICO CARUSO (1873–1921)

Hunger is the best sauce in the world.
MIGUEL DE CERVANTES (1547–1616)

An herb is the friend of physicians and the praise of cooks.
CHARLEMAGNE (742–814)

Pistachio nuts, the red ones, cure any problem.
PAULA DANZIGER (B. 1944)

[Cheese is] milk's leap toward immortality.
CLIFTON FADIMAN (B. 1904)

A hungry man is an angry man.
JAMES HOWELL (C. 1594–1666)

We never repent for having eaten too little.
THOMAS JEFFERSON (1743–1826)

Never eat more than you can lift.
MISS PIGGY (CREATED 1976 BY JIM HENSON AND FRANK OZ)

One should eat to live and not live to eat.
MOLIÈRE (1622–1673)

Honesty is the best policy and spinach is the best vegetable.
POPEYE (CREATED 1929 BY E. C. SEGAR)

[Some] Chinese mothers show they love their children,
not through hugs and kisses,
but with stern offerings of steamed dumplings.
AMY TAN (B. 1952)

SAYINGS THAT ARE
ABOUT MORE THAN FOOD

Too many cooks spoil the broth.
*Meaning: If too many experts work
on the same project, they will mess up the job.*
AMERICAN PROVERB

The proof of the pudding is in the eating.
*Meaning: Even if something looks good,
don't believe it is until you have checked it out yourself.*
MIGUEL DE CERVANTES (1547–1616)

One man's meat is another man's poison.
*Meaning: Everyone has different tastes.
What one person enjoys might seem terrible to someone else.*
ENGLISH PROVERB

It isn't so much what's on the table
that matters, as what's on the chairs.
Meaning: Who you share a meal with
is more important than what you eat.
W.S. GILBERT (1836–1911)

Better is half a loaf than no bread.
Meaning: Having something, even if its less than
what you had hoped for, is better than having nothing at all.
JOHN HEYWOOD (C. 1497–1580)

Cold rice and cold tea are bearable,
but cold looks and cold words are not.
Meaning: Eating cold food does you no real harm,
but being treated badly by others can really hurt you.
JAPANESE PROVERB

If you want to eat eggs, first take care of the hen.
Meaning: You must not expect anything
to come to you without planning and effort.
WEST AFRICAN PROVERB

WHO SAID, "LET THEM EAT CAKE"?

There have been times in history when wealthy, pampered rulers did not care about or understand the problems their poorest subjects faced. Legend says that when the French queen Marie Antoinette (1755–1793) learned that her subjects had no bread to eat, she responded with these words. However, she was not the first to use such a suggestion to show a lack of concern or knowledge of the needs of the hungry. She may have been quoting the French philospher Rousseau (1712–1778) or an earlier queen of France, Therese of Austria (1638–1683) since some historians say they used these words earlier. Others have expressed similar ideas under similar circumstances. Hundreds of years before, an emperor in China was told that his subjects did not have enough rice to eat. The emperor replied, "Why don't they eat meat?"

FREEDOM

Liberty cannot be preserved without
a general knowledge among the people.
JOHN ADAMS (1735–1826)

A people that loves freedom will in the end be free.
SIMÓN BOLÍVAR (1783–1830)

You can only protect your liberties in this world by protecting
the other man's freedom. You can only be free if I am free.
CLARENCE DARROW (1857–1938)

No man can put a chain about the ankle of his fellow man
without at least finding the other end of it about his own neck.
FREDERICK DOUGLASS (1817–1895)

Where liberty dwells, there is my country.
BENJAMIN FRANKLIN (1706–1790)

Liberty! Equality! Fraternity!
Liberté! Egalité! Fraternité!
(old motto officially adopted in 1793 as the motto
of the French Revolution and the new Republic)
FRENCH SAYING

I know not what course others may take,
but as for me, give me liberty or give me death!
PATRICK HENRY (1736–1799)

I have sworn upon the altar of God, eternal hostility
against every form of tyranny over the mind of man.
THOMAS JEFFERSON (1743–1926)

You might as well expect the rivers to run backward
as that any man who was born a free man should be contented
when penned up and denied liberty to go where he pleases.
CHIEF JOSEPH (HINMATON YALAKTIT) (1830–1904)

I have always thought that all men should be free;
but if any should be slaves, it should be first those who desire it
for themselves, and secondly those who desire it for others.
ABRAHAM LINCOLN (1809–1865)

Freedom is never given; it is won.
A. PHILIP RANDOLPH (1889–1979)

Liberty oh Liberty! What crimes are committed in your name!
(said before her execution)
MADAME ROLAND (1754–1793)

I had reasoned this out in my mind, there was two things
I had a right to: liberty and death. If I could not have one, I would
have the other, for no man should take me alive.
HARRIET TUBMAN (1815–1913)

I disapprove of what you say,
but I will defend to the death your right to say it.
VOLTAIRE (1694–1778)

Liberty, when it begins to take root is a plant of rapid growth.
GEORGE WASHINGTON (1732–1799)

FRIENDSHIP AND LOYALTY

"Stay" is a charming word in a friend's vocabulary.
LOUISA MAY ALCOTT (1832–1888)

He who has a thousand friends has not a friend to spare,
And he who has one enemy will meet him everywhere.
ALI (C. 602–661)

Make new friends, but keep the old.
One is silver, the other gold.
ANONYMOUS

A faithful friend is the medicine of life.
BIBLE: ECCLESIASTICUS 6:16

If we build on a sure foundation in friendship,
we must love our friends for their own sakes rather than our own.
CHARLOTTE BRONTË (1816–1855)

Even the best of friends must part.
GEOFFREY CHAUCER (C. 1343–1400)

Fate chooses our relatives, we choose our friends.
JACQUES DELILLE (1738–1813)

A friend in need is a friend indeed.
ENNIUS (239–169 B.C.)

To lose a friend, loan him money.
GREEK PROVERB

I like a friend better for having faults one can talk about.
WILLIAM HAZLITT (1778–1830)

Friend! It is a common word, often lightly used. Like other good
and beautiful things, it may be tarnished by careless handling.
HARRIET ANN JACOBS (1813–1897)

Old friends is always best, 'less you can catch
a new one that's fit to make an old one out of.
SARAH ORNE JEWETT (1849–1909)

Criticize a friend in private, but praise him in front of others.
LEONARDO DA VINCI (1452–1519)

A thousand friends are few; one enemy is too many.
RUSSIAN PROVERB

Be slow to fall into friendship, but when you have
be firm and constant in that friendship.
SOCRATES (469–399 B. C.)

He that is wise can make a friend of a foe.
SCOTTISH PROVERB

In choosing a friend, go up a step.
TALMUD

A good friend will fit you like a ring to a finger.
VENEZUELAN PROVERB

Laughter is not at all a bad beginning for a friendship.
OSCAR WILDE (1854–1900)

RALPH WALDO EMERSON: AN INFLUENTIAL FRIEND

Ralph Waldo Emerson (1803–1882) trained as a minister. He gave many lectures and published many essays and poems that passionately presented his ideas on life. Emerson's style is unmistakable. Using many proverbs and sayings gleaned from the past gave his work a certain style and rhythm. Even if his readers or listeners did not understand every point he made, they came away with quotable nuggets of wisdom. He counted among his friends several great writers and thinkers of his day, including Nathaniel Hawthorne, Henry David Thoreau, Louisa May Alcott and her father, Bronson, Oliver Wendell Holmes, Sr., and William Lloyd Garrison. The quotations below all come from Emerson's essay on friendship. Perhaps his conversations with these friends helped inspire the memorable words listed below.

A friend is a person with whom I may be sincere.
Before him I may think aloud.

The only way to have a friend is to be one.

A friend may well be reckoned
the masterpiece of nature.

FUTURE

You can never plan the future by the past.
EDMUND BURKE (1729–1797)

Who knows? Somewhere out in this audience may even be someone who will one day follow in my footsteps, and preside over the White House as the president's spouse. I wish him well!
BARBARA BUSH (B. 1925)

I never think of the future. It comes soon enough.
ALBERT EINSTEIN (1879–1955)

I have no way of judging the future but by the past.
PATRICK HENRY (1736–1799)

What will be, will be.
Che sera, sera.
ITALIAN PROVERB

My interest is in the future because
I'm going to spend the rest of my life there.
CHARLES F. KETTERING (1876–1958)

The Future [is] something that everyone reaches at the rate of
sixty minutes an hour, whatever he does, whatever he is.
C. S. LEWIS (1898–1963)

The best thing about the future is that it comes one day at a time.
ABRAHAM LINCOLN (1809–1865)

There was a Door through which I found no key.
There was a Veil through which I might not see.
OMAR KHAYYÁM (C. 1048–C. 1131)

In the future everyone will be world-famous for fifteen minutes.
ANDY WARHOL (1927–1987)

GOOD FORTUNE
AND MISFORTUNE

Don't trouble trouble till trouble troubles you.
AFRICAN-AMERICAN SAYING

Throw a lucky man into the sea,
and he will return with a fish in his mouth.
ARAB PROVERB

What is bad luck for one man is good luck for another.
ASHANTI PROVERB

Misfortunes will happen to the wisest and best of men.
What cannot be prevented should not be grieved for.
BIG ELK (C. 1772–1846)

If we had no winter, the spring would not be so pleasant,
if we did not sometimes taste of adversity,
prosperity would not be so welcome.
ANNE BRADSTREET (C. 1612–1672)

To a brave man, good luck and bad luck
are like his right and left hands. He uses both.
ST. CATHERINE OF SIENA (1347–1380)

With luck even a fool wins glory, without it a hero is helpless.
DANG DUNG (C. 1750)

Shallow men believe in luck.
RALPH WALDO EMERSON (1803–1882)

All good things come to those who wait.
ENGLISH PROVERB

April showers bring May flowers
ENGLISH PROVERB

Fortune favors the brave.
ENNIUS (239–169 B.C.)

True luck consists not in holding the best of the cards at the table:
Luckiest is he who knows just when to rise and go home.
JOHN HAY (1838–1905)

Everyone wants to share in a man's success,
but no one wants to share in his misfortunes.
INDIAN PROVERB

Little minds are tamed and subdued by misfortune;
but great minds rise above it.
WASHINGTON IRVING (1783–1859)

I am a great believer in luck, and I find
the harder I work the more I have of it.
STEPHEN LEACOCK (1869–1944)

He who does not try has no luck.
MEXICAN PROVERB

Lightning never strikes twice in the same place.
MARY ROBERTS RINEHART (1876–1958)

People always call it luck when you
act more sensibly than they have.
ANNE TYLER (B. 1941)

Don't sit down and wait for the opportunities to come.
You have to get up and make them.
MADAME C. J. WALKER (1867–1919)

Luck is a matter of preparation meeting opportunity.
OPRAH WINFREY (B. 1954)

GOVERNMENT AND POLITICS

Power tends to corrupt and absolute power corrupts absolutely.
Great men are almost always bad men.
LORD ACTON (1834–1902)

The good of man must be the goal of the science of politics.
ARISTOTLE (384–322 B.C.)

The great questions of the time are not decided by speeches and
majority decisions . . . but by iron and blood.
OTTO VON BISMARCK (1815–1898)

Regular elections are essential to maintain democracy.
There is nothing so dangerous as to allow power to remain for a
long time in one citizen. The people become accustomed
to obeying him and he becomes accustomed to commanding.
Hence the origin of tyranny.
SIMÓN BOLÍVAR (1783–1830)

The use of force alone is but *temporary* . . . and a nation
is not governed, which is perpetually to be conquered.
EDMUND BURKE (1729–1797)

The very essence of a free government consists in considering
offices as public trusts, bestowed for the good of the country,
and not for the benefit of an individual or a party.
JOHN C. CALHOUN (1782–1850)

No written law has ever been more binding than
unwritten custom supported by popular opinion.
CARRIE CHAPMAN CATT (1859–1947)

Political parties serve to keep each other in check,
one keenly watching the other.
HENRY CLAY (1777–1852)

Possession is nine parts of the law.
EDWARD III (1312–1377)

When we are sick, we want an uncommon doctor;
when we have a construction job to do, we want an uncommon
engineer, and when we are at war, we want an uncommon general.
It is only when we get into politics
that we are satisfied with the common man.
HERBERT HOOVER (1874–1964)

It may be true that the law cannot make a man love me, but it
can keep him from lynching me, and I think that is pretty important.
MARTIN LUTHER KING, JR. (1929–1968)

No man is good enough to govern another
without that other's consent.
ABRAHAM LINCOLN (1809–1865)

Wherever law ends, tyranny begins.
JOHN LOCKE (1632–1704)

Every nation has the government it deserves.
JOSEPH MARIE, COMTE DE MAISTRE (1753–1821)

The best form of government is that which is
most likely to prevent the greatest sum of evil.
JAMES MONROE (1758–1831)

In politics . . . you need two things: friends but above all an enemy.
BRIAN MULRONEY (B. 1939)

It is far better to be free to govern, or misgovern,
yourself than to be governed by anybody else.
KWAME NKRUMAH (1909–1972)

The essential ingredient in politics is timing.
PIERRE ELLIOTT TRUDEAU (B. 1919)

One uses what is right for today to govern the world of today,
but this does not mean that it will be right for a later day.
WANG FU-CHIH (1619–1692)

No republic ever yet stood on a stable foundation
without satisfying the common people.
MERCY OTIS WARREN (1728–1814)

THOMAS JEFFERSON ON GOVERNMENT

Thomas Jefferson (1743–1826) served two terms as president
of the United States but did not consider being president one
of his greatest accomplishments. He was proud of having drafted
the Declaration of Independence and Virginia's statute on
religious freedom as well as the role he played in founding the
University of Virginia.

Jefferson believed that informed and educated people would
use their knowledge to make wise decisions for their own and the
common good. He often presented the view that the best
government was the one that interfered the least with the ways
in which people chose to live their lives.

We hold these truths to be self-evident,
that all men are created equal, that they are endowed
by their Creator with certain unalienable rights,
that among these are life, liberty and the pursuit of happiness.
Whenever any form of government
becomes destructive of these ends,
it is the right of the people to alter or to abolish it.
(*from the Declaration of Independence*)

Were it left to me to decide whether we should have a
government without newspapers, or newspapers without a
government, I should not hesitate a moment to prefer the latter.

Error of opinion may be tolerated
where reason is left free to combat it.

The whole of government consists in the art of being honest.

I hold it, that a little rebellion, now and then,
is a good thing, and as necessary in the political world
as storms in the physical {world}.
(*said of Shays's Rebellion, 1786*)

That government is best which governs the least,
because its people discipline themselves.

When a man assumes a public trust
he should consider himself public property.

GREATNESS

Great minds think alike.
AMERICAN PROVERB

Nurture your mind with great thoughts.
To believe in the heroic makes heroes.
BENJAMIN DISRAELI (1804–1881)

If a man write a better book, preach a better sermon,
or make a better mousetrap, than his neighbor,
though he build his house in the woods,
the world will make a beaten path to his door.
RALPH WALDO EMERSON (1803–1882)

From the sublime to the ridiculous is but a step.
FRENCH PROVERB

The idol of today pushed the hero of yesterday out of our recollection;
and will, in turn be supplanted by [a new hero] tomorrow.
WASHINGTON IRVING (1783–1859)

Great oaks from little acorns grow.
LATIN PROVERB

Lives of great men all remind us
We can make our lives sublime.
And departing, leave behind us
Footprints in the sands of time.
HENRY WADSWORTH LONGFELLOW (1807–1882)

If fame is to come only after death, I am in no hurry for it.
MARTIAL (MARCUS VALERIUS MARTIALIS) (A.D. C. 40–C. 104)

He who has never failed cannot be great.
Failure is the true test of greatness.
HERMAN MELVILLE (1819–1891)

The great man is he who has the heart of a child.
MENCIUS (MENG-TZU) (372–289 B.C.)

Those who aim at great deeds must also suffer greatly.
PLUTARCH (A.D. 46–120)

Be not afraid of greatness: some are born great, some achieve
greatness, and some have greatness thrust upon them.
WILLIAM SHAKESPEARE (1564–1616)

Appreciation is a wonderful thing:
it makes what is excellent in others belong to us as well.
VOLTAIRE (1694–1778)

HAPPINESS AND SORROW

Rejoice with them that rejoice, and weep with them that weep.
BIBLE: ROMANS 12:15

Happiness comes when your work and your words
are of benefit to yourself and to others.
BUDDHA (C. 563–483 B.C.)

Success is getting what you want.
Happiness is wanting what you get.
DALE CARNEGIE (1888–1955)

A day of sorrow is longer than a month of joy.
CHINESE PROVERB

The entire world weeps for me.
CHIPPEWA SONG

My opinion is that you never find happiness
until you stop looking for it.
CHUANG-TZU (369–286 B.C.)

A kitten is a child's happiness.
CUBAN PROVERB

The Constitution only guarantees the American people
the right to pursue happiness—you have to catch it yourself.
BENJAMIN FRANKLIN (1706–1790)

A happy heart is better than a full purse.
ITALIAN PROVERB

Misery loves company.
PUBLILIUS SYRUS (1ST CENTURY B.C.)

Happiness lies not in the mere possession of money.
It lies in the joy of achievement, in the thrill of creative effort.
FRANKLIN ROOSEVELT (1882–1945)

Happiness is a warm puppy.
CHARLES SCHULZ (B. 1922)

How bitter a thing it is to look at happiness
through another man's eyes!
WILLIAM SHAKESPEARE (1564–1616)

Parting is such sweet sorrow.
(Romeo to Juliet)
WILLIAM SHAKESPEARE (1564–1616)

The greater part of any happiness or misery depends on
our dispositions and not on our circumstances.
MARTHA WASHINGTON (1731–1802)

HEALTH

Laughter is the best medicine.
AMERICAN TRADITION

One reason I don't drink is that
I want to know when I am having a good time.
NANCY ASTOR (1879–1964)

As to diseases make a habit of two things—
to help, or at least, to do no harm.
HIPPOCRATES (C. 460–377 B.C.)

You should pray for a sound mind in a sound body.
JUVENAL (A.D. C. 55–C. 130)

If you go long enough without a bath,
even the fleas will let you alone.
ERNIE PYLE (1900–1945)

Just say no [to drugs].
NANCY REAGAN (B. 1923)

To a sick man even honey tastes bitter.
RUSSIAN PROVERB

Health is . . . a blessing that money cannot buy.
IZAAK WALTON (1593–1683)

An apple a day keeps the doctor away.
WELSH PROVERB

HELPING AND KINDNESS

Put your shoulder to the wheel. . . .
The gods help them that help themselves.
AESOP (FL. C. 550 B.C.)

If you have much, give of your wealth.
If you have little, give of your heart.
ARAB PROVERB

The quickest generosity is the best.
ARAB PROVERB

For even in dreams a good deed is not lost.
PEDRO CALDERÓN DE LA BARCA (1600–1681)

Shall we make a new rule of life . . .
always to try to be a little kinder than is necessary?
J. M. BARRIE (1860–1937)

It is more blessed to give than to receive.
BIBLE: ACTS 20:35

Give a man a fish and you feed him for a day.
Teach a man to fish and you feed him for a lifetime.
CHINESE PROVERB

No one is useless in this world who lightens the burden of others.
CHARLES DICKENS (1812–1870)

When one helps another, both gain in strength.
ECUADORIAN PROVERB

It is quite fitting that charity should begin at home . . .
but then it should not end at home; for those that
help nobody will find none to help them in time of need.
MARIA EDGEWORTH (1767–1849)

You give but little when you give of your possessions.
It is when you give of yourself that you truly give.
KAHLIL GIBRAN (1883–1931)

No matter what accomplishment you make, somebody helps you.
ALTHEA GIBSON (B. 1927)

When you clench your fist, no one can put anything in your hand.
ALEX HALEY (1921–1992)

One kind word can warm three winter months.
JAPANESE PROVERB

No good deed goes unpunished.
CLARE BOOTHE LUCE (1903–1987)

Kindness is a mark of faith;
and whoever hath not kindness, hath not faith.
MUHAMMAD (570–632)

HISTORY

We must be the authors of the history of our age.
MADELINE ALBRIGHT (B. 1937)

History repeats itself.
ANONYMOUS

Solemn history, I cannot be interested in . . .
the quarrels of popes and kings, with wars and pestilences
on every page, . . . and hardly any women at all.
JANE AUSTEN (1775–1817)

When they learn about Caesar and his legions,
we must [also] teach them of Hannibal and his Africans.
MARY MCLEOD BETHUNE (1875–1955)

What is not recorded is not remembered.
BENAZIR BHUTTO (B. 1953)

The first law for the historian is that he shall never dare to speak a lie.
The second is that he shall hide nothing that is true.
CICERO (106–43 B.C.)

History shows us that nothing is often
a good thing to do and always a good thing to say.
WILL DURANT (1885–1981) AND
ARIEL DURANT (1898–1981)

History teaches us that men and nations behave wisely
once they have exhausted all other possibilities.
ABBA EBAN (B. 1915)

People, human beings with all their creative diversity,
are the makers of history.
MIKHAIL GORBACHEV (B. 1931)

Those who cannot remember the past are condemned to repeat it.
GEORGE SANTAYANA (1863–1952)

Wherever men have lived there is a story to be told,
and it depends chiefly on the story-teller or historian
whether it is interesting or not.
HENRY DAVID THOREAU (1817–1862)

What we need is not a history of selected races or nations,
but the history of the world void of national bias,
race hate, and religious prejudice.
CARTER WOODSON (1875–1950)

"It was the best of times, it was the worst of times."
*Meaning: Noble actions and ideals can exist side by side
or entwined with bad intentions and outcomes.*

These words begin the opening sentence of *A Tale of Two Cities*. Charles Dickens (1812–1870) wrote this novel about the French Revolution (1789–1799), when the people rose up against their king and the noblemen who helped govern by right of their birth. The people of France wanted a democracy—that was good. However, some corrupt people misused the power of the Revolutionary tribunal—and that was very bad. Many innocent people were sentenced to death by guillotine or died when mobs rioted. It took many years before France had peace and a stable government.

The story that Dickens told was historical fiction, but it was also meant as a cautionary tale for his own time. Dickens worried that England would have a revolution if reforms were not enacted to help the English government become more responsive to the needs of the people.

Fortunately for Dickens and for England, Queen Victoria realized that the English monarchy had to give up some of its power to survive. She let Parliament and its ministers take more authority. England had the changes it needed without a revolution.

HOME

The ache for home lives in all of us,
the safe place where we can go and not be questioned.
MAYA ANGELOU (B. 1928)

There is nothing like staying home for real comfort.
JANE AUSTEN (1775–1817)

My home is humble and unattractive to strangers, but to me
it contains what I shall find nowhere else in the world—
the . . . affection which brothers and sisters feel for each other.
CHARLOTTE BRONTË (1816–1855)

The house of everyone is to him as his castle and fortress.
SIR EDWARD COKE (1552–1634)

Where thou art, that is home.
EMILY DICKINSON (1830–1886)

Home is where one starts from.
T. S. ELIOT (1888–1965)

He is happiest, be he king or peasant,
who finds peace in his own home.
JOHANN WOLFGANG VON GOETHE (1749–1832)

It takes a heap o' livin' in a house t' make it home.
EDGAR GUEST (1881–1959)

Bricks and mortar make a house,
but the laughter of children makes a home.
IRISH PROVERB

A house is a machine for living in.
LE CORBUSIER (1887–1965)

A man travels the world over in search of
what he needs and returns home to find it.
GEORGE MOORE (1852–1933)

Be it ever so humble, there's no place like home.
JOHN PAYNE (1791–1852)

Home is where the heart is.
PLINY THE ELDER (A.D. 23–79)

I had three chairs in my house: one for solitude,
two for friendship, three for society.
HENRY DAVID THOREAU (1817–1862)

HUMAN NATURE

Familiarity breeds contempt.
*Meaning: when we know people well,
we learn their faults and lose respect for them.*
AESOP (FL. C. 550 B.C.)

Man is by nature a political animal.
ARISTOTLE (384–322 B.C.)

What you really value is what you miss, not what you have.
JORGE LUIS BORGES (1899–1986)

Man's inhumanity to man
Makes countless thousands mourn!
ROBERT BURNS (1759–1796)

Each human is uniquely different.
Like snowflakes, the human pattern is never cast twice.
ALICE CHILDRESS (1920–1994)

Human nature is the same everywhere.
LORD CHESTERFIELD (1694–1773)

What is told in the ear of a man is often heard 100 miles away.
CHINESE SAYING

In spite of everything I still believe that
people are really good at heart.
ANNE FRANK (1929–1945)

It is to the credit of human nature ...
that it loves more readily than it hates.
NATHANIEL HAWTHORNE (1804–1864)

The great masses of the people ... will more easily
fall victims to a big lie than to a small one.
ADOLF HITLER (1889–1945)

There never were in the world, two opinions alike.
Their most universal quality is diversity.
MICHEL DE MONTAIGNE (1533–1592)

To err is human, to forgive divine.
ALEXANDER POPE (1688–1744)

WILL ROGERS: AN OBSERVER OF HUMAN NATURE

Entertainer Will Rogers (1879–1935) grew up in Oklahoma.
He was proud of his Cherokee ancestry and his early years
as a cowboy. Rogers was one of the most popular authors,
lecturers, and humorists of his time. His career began when he
joined Texas Jack's Wild West Show as a trick roper. He began
telling jokes as he did his tricks. His humor was based on a
common sense approach to life and a basic affection and respect
for all people. He said:

I joked about every prominent man in my lifetime,
but I never met one I didn't like.

We are all ignorant. Only about different things.

Everything is funny as long as it is
happening to somebody else.

HUMOR

He is not laughed at who laughs at himself first.
AMERICAN TRADITION

Laughter is the shortest distance between two people.
VICTOR BORGE (B. 1909)

A good pun may be admitted among the
smaller excellencies of lively conversation.
JAMES BOSWELL (1749–1795)

The most wasted day of all is that on which we have not laughed.
SÉBASTIEN ROCH NICOLAS CHAMFORT (1741–1794)

Laugh, and the world laughs with you; weep and you weep alone.
ELLA WHEELER WILCOX (1850–1919)

He laughs best who laughs last.
JOHN HEYWOOD (C. 1497–C. 1580)

Humor is laughing at what you haven't got
when you ought to have it.
LANGSTON HUGHES (1902–1967)

He deserves paradise who makes his companions laugh.
THE KORAN

You bet being funny helps accomplish things.
I've always maintained that people don't realize how many
brain cells it takes to be funny. And politics ought to be fun—
after baseball it's our next favorite national pastime.
ANN RICHARDS (B. 1933)

A jest's prosperity lies in the ear
Of him who hears it, never in the tongue
Of him who makes it.
WILLIAM SHAKESPEARE (1564–1616)

Whatever else an American believes or disbelieves about himself,
he is absolutely sure he has a sense of humor.
E. B. WHITE (1899–1985)

MARK TWAIN CREATES HUMOR

Samuel Langhorne Clemens (1835–1910) used the pen name Mark Twain when he wrote *The Adventures of Huckleberry Finn* and many other books. The powerful stories he told and the humor he used to tell them made Clemens one of the most popular authors of his day. Since he was a shy, private person, Clemens solved the problem of what to do when asked to appear in public by playing Twain as an actor would a character in a show. Mark Twain was even funnier and more outrageous in person than he was on the printed page, and some of his funniest quotes come from quips he made during public appearances.

Man is the only animal that blushes. Or needs to.

When I was a boy of fourteen, my father was so ignorant
I could hardly stand to have the old man around.
But when I got to be twenty-one, I was astonished at
how much he had learned in seven years.

Nothing so needs reforming
as other people's habits.

JUSTICE AND EQUALITY

Civilization is a method of living,
an attitude of equal respect for all men.
JANE ADDAMS (1860–1935)

What goes around comes around.
AFRICAN-AMERICAN SAYING

Finders keepers, losers weepers.
AMERICAN PROVERB

There will never be complete equality until women themselves
help to make the laws and elect lawmakers.
SUSAN B. ANTHONY (1820–1906)

Mercy to the criminal may be cruelty to the people.
ARAB PROVERB

Law is order, and good laws make for good order.
ARISTOTLE (384–322 B.C.)

An unjust law is no law at all.
SAINT AUGUSTINE (354–430)

America did not invent human rights.
In a very real sense human rights invented America.
JIMMY CARTER (B. 1924)

The fight is never about grapes or lettuce.
It is always about people.
CESAR CHAVEZ (1927–1993)

Let the punishment match the offense.
CICERO (106–43 B.C.)

Justice is truth in action.
BENJAMIN DISRAELI (1804–1881)

A man is innocent until proven guilty.
ENGLISH COMMON LAW

First come, first served.
ENGLISH PROVERB

Justice is a machine that, when someone has
once given it a starting push, rolls on of itself.
JOHN GALSWORTHY (1867–1933)

These are the laws of justice. . . . That the strong may not oppress the weak, to give justice to the orphan and the widow.

HAMMURABI (D. 1750 B.C.)

Do not judge your fellow man until you have stood in his place.

HILLEL (FL. 30 B.C.–A.D. 10)

The sword of murder is not the balance of justice.
Blood does not wipe out dishonor,
nor violence indicate possession.

JULIA WARD HOWE (1819–1910)

Righteousness means justice practiced
between men and between nations.

IROQUOIS TRADITION

It is more dangerous that even a guilty person should be punished without the forms of law than that he should escape.

THOMAS JEFFERSON (1743–1826)

The earth is the mother of all people,
and all people should have equal rights upon it.

JOSEPH (HINMATON-YALAKTIT) (C. 1840–1904)

The moment you have protected the individual
you have protected society.

KENNETH KANUDA (B. 1924)

Justice is blind.
LATIN PROVERB

Peace was not made for the sake of justice,
but justice for the sake of peace.
MARTIN LUTHER (1483–1546)

Chivalry is a poor substitute for justice, if one cannot have both.
Chivalry is something like the icing on the cake,
sweet but not nourishing.
NELLIE McCLUNG (1873–1951)

No one should be judge in his own case.
PUBLILIUS SYRUS (1ST CENTURY B.C.)

Nations will rise and fall but equality remains the ideal.
The universal aim is to achieve respect for entire human race.
CARLOS PEÑA ROMULO (1899–1985)

Justice is conscience . . . the conscience of the whole of humanity.
Those who clearly recognize the voice of their own consciences
usually recognize also the voice of justice.
ALEXANDER SOLZHENITSYN (B. 1918)

I do not wish [women] to have power over men;
but over themselves.
MARY WOLLSTONECRAFT (1759–1797)

LANGUAGE AND WORDS

All words are pegs to hang ideas on.
HENRY WARD BEECHER [1813–1887)

By thy words thou shalt be justified,
and by thy words thou shalt be condemned.
BIBLE: MATTHEW 12:37

Words can do wonderful things.
They can urge; they can wheedle, whip or whine.
They can forge a fiery army out of a hundred languid men.
GWENDOLYN BROOKS (B. 1917)

The pen is mightier than the sword.
EDWARD GEORGE BULWER-LYTTON (1803–1873)

Speech is silver; silence is golden.
THOMAS CARLYLE (1795–1881)

Do not speak ill of the dead.
DIOGENES (C. 400–C. 325 B.C.)

A word is dead
When it is said,
Some say.
I say it just
Begins to live
That day.
EMILY DICKINSON (1830–1886)

Do not tell secrets to those whose faith and silence
you have not already tested.
ELIZABETH I (1533–1603)

Provoking, isn't it? That when one is most in need of
sensible words, one finds them not.
CHARLOTTE FORTEN GRIMKÉ (1837–1914)

All foods are good to eat, but not all words are fit to speak.
HAITIAN PROVERB

Let poetry be like a key
Opening a thousand doors.
VICENTE HUIDOBRO (1893–1948)

I quote others to better express myself.
MICHEL DE MONTAIGNE (1533–1592)

Spoken words are living things, like cocoa-beans packed with life.
And like cocoa-beans they grow and give life.
GABRIEL OKARA (B. 1921)

What is well said by another is mine.
LUCIUS ANNAEUS SENECA (C. 4 B.C.–A.D. 65)

Bright is the ring of words
When the right man rings them.
ROBERT LOUIS STEVENSON (1850–1894)

The difference between the *almost*-right word & the *right* word
is really a large matter—it's the difference between
the lightning bug and the lightning.

MARK TWAIN (1835–1910)

WHAT'S IN A NAME...?
SHAKESPEARE MAKES HIS MARK
UPON THE ENGLISH LANGUAGE

William Shakespeare (1564–1616) was an English playwright and poet. He was also an actor whose living depended upon the success of his plays on the stage. He dedicated the poetry he published to wealthy patrons of the arts whom he hoped would sponsor his work. He never dreamed that centuries after his death he would be one of the most often-quoted authors in the world, and one of the most widely-read.

Words and phrases from Shakespeare's works have become part of everyday speech. For example, Shakespeare was the first to use the words *amazement*, *bump*, *successful,* and *lonely*; and the phrases *wild-goose chase* and *fair play*. Shakespeare also took old proverbs and old stories and added his own touches to make them his own. Before writing his play *Julius Caesar*, Shakepeare read an English translation of Plutarch's life of Caesar. Plutarch described how Caesar was warned to "take heed of the ides [the fifteenth day] of March." Shakespeare improved upon Plutarch to come up with the much more dramatic, and quotable, "Beware the ides of March."

Some of Shakespeare's popular quotations are easy to understand on their own, but others are puzzling unless you know something about Shakespearean vocabulary and the play from which they come. Here are some favorite quotes explained:

All the world's a stage,
And all the men and women merely players.
Meaning: The world is like a theater and its people are only actors, playing out roles. A gloomy character named Jaques recites this in the play As You Like It. *He uses these words to introduce his thoughts on what people do at different ages in their life from "mewling {crying} and puking" when they are babies to declining at the end of life into "second childishness and mere oblivion."*

Brevity is the soul of wit.
Meaning: Clever speakers manage to say a lot with a few words. Shakespeare added humor to a scene from Hamlet *when he had a character named Polonious use these words as part of a long, rambling talk.*

Double, double toil and trouble
Fire burn, and cauldron bubble.
Meaning: This comes from a scene in which three witches are stirring up a brew to bring misfortune to a man named Macbeth. When people use these words today they mean that someone is "stirring up" trouble.

A horse, a horse! My kingdom for a horse!
Meaning: These words are spoken by King Richard III when his horse has died and he himself is about to meet his doom in battle with the man who will soon replace him as king. When people

quote these lines from Richard III *they are talking about a desire to keep going even though they are facing an unbeatable situation.*

To be, or not to be: that is the question.
Meaning: Used today when a speaker wants to suggest that he or she is not sure which choice to make, these words were first said in the play Hamlet *by the title character, the troubled prince of Denmark, who is trying to decide whether it would be better to end his life or go on living. (He decides to live.)*

What's in a name? that which we call a rose
By any other word would smell as sweet.
Meaning: The name of a person does not matter; a person's qualities and actions are what matters. In Romeo and Juliet, *Juliet uses these words when she speaks to her Romeo, explaining that she loves him despite the fact that their families are sworn enemies.*

LEADERS AND LEADERSHIP

Authority without wisdom is like a heavy axe
without an edge, fitter to bruise than polish.
ANNE BRADSTREET (C. 1612–1672)

I praise loudly. I blame softly.
CATHERINE II (1729–1796)

In my position you have to read when you want to write and
to talk when you would like to read. You have to laugh when you
feel like crying. . . . You have no time for a moment's thought,
and nevertheless you have to be constantly ready to act.
CATHERINE II (1729–1796)

It is easy to get a thousand soldiers, but difficult to get a general.
CHINESE PROVERB

I believe that women have a special contribution to make . . .
because they have special qualities of leadership
which are greatly needed today. And these qualities
are patience, tolerance, and perseverance.
SHIRLEY CHISHOLM (B. 1924)

For everyone called to the government of nations and empires,
[he must] show himself as a father of the common people.
CONFUCIUS (551–479 B.C.)

I suppose leadership at one time meant muscles;
but today it means getting along with people.
INDIRA GANDHI (1917–1984)

My command stands firm like the mountains.
HATSHEPSUT (1503–1482 B.C.)

I want there to be no peasant in my realm so poor
that he will not have a chicken in his pot every Sunday.
HENRI IV (HENRY OF NAVARRE) (1553–1610)

A President's hardest task is not to do what is right,
but to know what is right.
LYNDON B. JOHNSON (1908–1973)

A leader is at his best when people barely know he exists.
When his work is done and his goal reached,
the others all say, "we did it ourselves."
LAO-TZU (604–531 B.C.)

Men are like the stars, some generate their own light
while others reflect the brilliance they receive.
JOSÉ MARTI (1853–1895)

Words like "leadership," "resolve," and "determination" are just
words until they are brought to life by men and women who dedicate
themselves . . . to the security and well-being of the nation.
COLIN POWELL (B. 1937)

Without a shepherd, sheep are not a flock.
RUSSIAN PROVERB

Uneasy lies the head that wears the crown.
WILLIAM SHAKESPEARE (1564–1616)

The queens of history compare favorably with the kings.
ELIZABETH CADY STANTON (1815–1902)

I never give answers. I lead on from one question
to another. That is my leadership.
RABINDRANATH TAGORE (1861–1941)

> ## SPEAK SOFTLY AND CARRY
> ## A BIG STICK; YOU WILL GO FAR
> *Meaning: Don't brag or threaten, but make sure you have
> the ability to use force if necessary; you will then succeed.*
>
> This saying is based on an old West African proverb and was
> popularized by President Theodore Roosevelt (1858-1919).
> The first time he used it in a public speech was in 1901. Roosevelt
> was serving as vice president and was speaking about United
> States foreign policy and the importance of maintaining a well-
> equipped and well-trained navy. A few months later, President
> William McKinley was felled by an assassin's bullet. Roosevelt
> became president and "Speak softly and carry a big stick" became
> his motto. It represented his philosophy of leadership at home in
> the United States as well as with the rest of the world.

LONELINESS AND SOLITUDE

Alas, the journey of life is beset with thorns
to those who must travel it alone.
ALEXANDRE DUMAS (1802–1870)

There is nothing so painful in the whole world
as feeling that one is not liked.
SEI SHŌNAGON (966–1013)

Loneliness is the most terrible poverty.
MOTHER TERESA (1910–1997)

I would rather sit on a pumpkin and have it all to myself
than be crowded on a velvet cushion.
HENRY DAVID THOREAU (1817–1862)

I'm so lonesome I could cry.
(*from song "I'm So Lonesome I Could Cry"*)
HANK WILLIAMS (1923–1953)

I wandered lonely as a cloud
That floats on high o'er vales and hills,
When all at once I saw a crowd,
A host, of golden daffodils.
WILLIAM WORDSWORTH (1770–1850)

LOVE AND HATE

Hatred stirreth up strifes: but love covereth all sins.
BIBLE: PROVERBS 10:12

Love your enemies.
BIBLE: MATTHEW 5:44

For me, to live without hate is easy,
for I have never felt hate. To live without love
I think is impossible, happily impossible, for each one of us.
JORGE LUIS BORGES (1899–1986)

There is . . . no Shark like hatred.
DHAMMAPADA (C. 3RD CENTURY)

I was in love with the whole world
and all that lived in its rainy arms.
LOUISE ERDRICH (B. 1954)

Love makes the world go round.
FRENCH PROVERB

At one glance
I love you
With a thousand hearts.
MIHRI HATUN (D. 1506)

Men's hatreds generally spring from fear and envy.
NICCOLÒ MACHIAVELLI (1469–1527)

It is far safer to be feared than to be loved,
when you have to choose between the two.
NICCOLÒ MACHIAVELLI (1469–1527)

True love is a durable fire,
In the mind ever burning.
SIR WALTER RALEGH (C. 1552–1618)

'Tis better to have loved and lost
Than never to have loved at all.
ALFRED, LORD TENNYSON (1809–1892)

Nothing can be either loved or hated unless it is first understood.
LEONARDO DA VINCI (1452–1519)

"HOW DO I LOVE THEE? LET ME COUNT THE WAYS"

Many poets have written words of love, but the most often quoted love poem starts with the question "How do I love thee?" These famous words begin a poem in which the poet goes on to list the many ways in which she loves her husband. Elizabeth Barrett Browning (1806–1861) used these words to begin the 43rd poem in a collection of poems called *Sonnets from the Portuguese* (1850).

Elizabeth Barrett was educated at home by her father, who recognized that his daughter was a talented writer and arranged for a poem of hers to be published when she was only 13. Her father, however, worried that Elizabeth was delicate and weak. She injured her spine in a fall when she was 15 and in her 20s and 30s her health worsened. She seldom left home and met few people, although she continued to write and publish her poetry. Then in 1844 she began receiving letters from another poet, a young man named Robert Browning, who admired her work. Robert Browning was to change her life. They met and became engaged in 1845. Elizabeth's father tried to stop the couple from marrying, saying his daughter was too ill to marry. But Elizabeth and Robert proved her father wrong. They married and moved to Italy, where her health improved greatly and they shared a full and happy life.

MANNERS

If a man be gracious and courteous to strangers, it shows that he is a citizen of the world, and this his heart is no island cut off from other lands, but a continent that joins to them.
FRANCIS BACON (1561–1626)

Learn politeness from the impolite.
EGYPTIAN PROVERB

There is always a best way of doing everything, if it be to boil an egg. Manners are the happy way of doing things.
RALPH WALDO EMERSON (1803–1882)

When in Rome, do as the Romans do.
ENGLISH PROVERB

Good behavior is everybody's business, and good taste can be everyone's goal.
MILLICENT FENWICK (1910–1992)

Rudeness is the weak man's imitation of strength.
ERIC HOFFER (1902–1983)

Adorable children are considered to be the general property of the whole human race. Rude children belong to their mothers.
JUDITH MARTIN ("MISS MANNERS") (B. 1938)

Civility costs nothing and buys everything.
LADY MARY WORTLEY MONTAGU (1689–1762)

Frame your manners to the time.
WILLIAM SHAKESPEARE (1564–1616)

Silence was meaningful with the Lakota and his granting a space of silence to the speech-maker and his own moment of silence before talking was done in the practice of true politeness.
LUTHER STANDING BEAR (1868–1939)

Children act in the village as they have learned at home.
SWEDISH PROVERB

In the presence of others sing not to yourself with a humming noise, nor drum with your fingers or your feet.
(*from his* Rules of Civility and Decent Behavior,
written when he was 15)
GEORGE WASHINGTON (1732–1799)

MATHEMATICS

Let no one enter here who does not know geometry [mathematics].
(*Inscribed over Plato's door at the Academy at Athens.*)
ANONYMOUS

An equation is something for eternity.
ALBERT EINSTEIN (1879–1955)

I am sorry to say that I dislike mathematics....I think
the reason is that mathematics leaves no room for argument.
If you made a mistake, that was all there was to it.
MALCOLM X (1925–1965)

Arithmetic is numbers you squeeze from your
head to your hand to your pencil to your paper
till you get the right answer.
CARL SANDBURG (1878–1967)

The science of pure mathematics ... may claim to be
the most original creation of the human spirit.
ALFRED NORTH WHITEHEAD (1861–1947)

MUSIC

All music is folk music.
LOUIS ARMSTRONG (1901–1971)

Opera is where a guy gets stabbed in the back,
and instead of dying he sings.
ROBERT BENCHLEY (1889–1945)

My music reaches to the sky.
CHIPPEWA SONG

Music hath charms to soothe a savage breast,
To soften rocks, or bend a knotted oak.
WILLIAM CONGREVE (1670–1729)

If I had my life to live over again, I would make a rule
to read some poetry and listen to some music....
The loss of these tastes is a loss of happiness and
may possibly be injurious to the intellect.
CHARLES DARWIN (1809–1892)

The only thing better than singing is more singing.
ELLA FITZGERALD (1917–1996)

True music... must repeat the thought and inspirations
of the people and the time. My people are Americans.
My time is today.
GEORGE GERSHWIN (1898–1937)

Of all the musical instruments the human voice
is the most beautiful, for it is made by God.
SHUSHA GUPPY (B. 1938)

The best way to get to know any bunch of people
is to go and listen to their music.
WOODY GUTHRIE (1912–1967)

Music expresses that which cannot be said and
on which it is impossible to be silent.
VICTOR HUGO (1802–1885)

Of all noises, I think music is the least disagreeable.
SAMUEL JOHNSON (1709–1784)

Music is the universal language of mankind.
HENRY WADSWORTH LONGFELLOW (1807–1882)

When I give a concert, I like to think that
I'm welcoming somebody to my home.
YO-YO MA (B. 1955)

Music is your own experience, your thoughts, your wisdom.
If you do not live it, it won't come through your horn.
CHARLIE PARKER (1920–1955)

I always believed that the right song
at the right moment could change history.
PETE SEEGER (B. 1919)

The man that hath no music in himself, . . .
Let no such man be trusted.
WILLIAM SHAKESPEARE (1564–1616)

Music, when soft voices die,
Vibrates in the memory. . . .
PERCY BYSSHE SHELLEY (1792–1822)

To hear [Mozart's] music is to feel
one has accomplished some good deed.
PYOTR ILICH TCHAIKOVSKY (1840–1893)

Yams fill the belly, but music fills the heart.
WEST AFRICAN PROVERB

NATURE

Nature does nothing uselessly.
ARISTOTLE (384–322 B.C.)

Learn about a pine tree from a pine tree
and a bamboo plant from a bamboo plant.
MATSUO BASHŌ (1644–1694)

We look too much to museums.
The sun coming up in the morning is enough.
ROMARE BEARDEN (1914–1988)

Consider the lilies of the field, how they grow;
they toil not, neither do they spin. Even Solomon
in all his glory was not arrayed like one of these.
BIBLE: MATTHEW 6:28–29

Hurt not the earth, neither the sea, nor the trees.
BIBLE: REVELATION 7:3

You shall not pollute the land in which you live.
BIBLE: NUMBERS 35:33

When we go hunting, it is not our arrow that kills the moose,
however powerful the bow; it is nature that kills him.
BIG THUNDER [BEDAGI] (LATE 19TH CENTURY)

The power of the world always works in circles,
and everything tries to be round. . . . The sky is round,
and I have heard that the earth is round like a ball,
and so are the stars. The wind, in its greatest power whirls.
Birds make their nests in circles. . . . Even the seasons
form a great circle in their changing and always
come back again to where they were.
BLACK ELK (HEHAKA SAPA) (1863–1950)

Like music and art, love of nature is a common language
that can transcend political and social boundaries.
JIMMY CARTER (B. 1924)

Nature is the art of God.
DANTE (1265–1321)

What is a weed?
A plant whose virtues have not yet been discovered.
RALPH WALDO EMERSON (1803–1882)

One outstanding important fact regarding Spaceship Earth,
and that is that no instruction manual came with it.
BUCKMINSTER FULLER (1895–1983)

All of the sounds of the earth are like music.
(from "Oh, What a Beautiful Mornin'")
OSCAR HAMMERSTEIN II (1895–1960)

Though you drive Nature out with a pitchfork,
she will always find her way back.
Naturum expellas furca, tamen usque recurret.
HORACE (65–8 B.C.)

Summer afternoon—summer afternoon;
to me those have always been the two most
beautiful words in the English language.
HENRY JAMES (1843–1916)

I think that I shall never see
A poem lovely as a tree.
JOYCE KILMER (1886–1918)

If a tree dies, plant another in its place.
CAROLUS LINNAEUS [CARL VON LINNÉ] (1707–1778)

Every formula which expresses a law of nature
is a hymn of praise to God.
MARIA MITCHELL (1818–1889)

There is a perfect freedom in the mountains,
but it belongs to the eagle, the elk, the badger, and the bear.
N. SCOTT MOMADAY (B. 1934)

All Nature's wildness tells the same story—
the shocks and outbursts of earthquakes, volcanoes, geysers, . . .
storms of every sort—each and all are the
beauty-making love-beats of Nature's heart.
JOHN MUIR (1838–1914)

One day in the country
Is worth a month in town.
CHRISTINA ROSSETTI (1830–1894)

Nature never deceives us; it is always we who deceive ourselves.
JEAN JACQUES ROUSSEAU (1712–1778)

Whatever befalls the Earth also befalls
the sons and daughters of the Earth.
CHIEF SEATTLE (C. 1786–1866)

All things in nature have an outward shape...
that is to say a form... whether it be the sweeping eagle in
his flight... [or] the winding river. Form ever follows function.
Where function does not change, form does not change.
LOUIS SULLIVAN (1856–1924)

You must not... be too precise or scientific about birds,
trees and flowers. A certain free margin...
helps your enjoyment of these things.
WALT WHITMAN (1819–1892)

The Earth is our mother.
The trees and all of nature are witnesses of her deeds.
WINNEBAGO TRADITIONAL

RACHEL CARSON'S WORDS
HELP SAVE THE ENVIRONMENT

Rachel Carson (1907–1964) always loved the sea, animals, and writing. Working as a marine biologist, she realized that pesticides, pollution, and other human activities were putting all life on Earth in danger. Because Carson was a gifted writer as well as a respected scientist, she was able to inspire people to take action. Her book *Silent Spring* (1962) became a best-seller. President John F. Kennedy and other government officials quoted her book in Congress and began to take action to pass laws to protect the environment. Here are some memorable words from her books on nature and the environment:

> Over increasingly large areas of the United States . . .
> the early mornings are strangely silent where once
> they were filled with the beauty of bird song.

> In every grain of sand there is a story of the earth.

> No witchcraft, no enemy action had silenced
> the rebirth of new life in this stricken world.
> The people had done it themselves.

> The "control of nature" is a phrase conceived
> in arrogance . . . when it was supposed that
> nature exists for the convenience of man.

NEWS AND THE MEDIA

One picture is worth a thousand words.
FRED BARNARD (C.1927)

As cold waters to a thirsty soul, so is good news from a far country.
BIBLE: PROVERBS 25:25

Four hostile newspapers are more
to be feared than a thousand bayonets.
NAPOLEON I (NAPOLEON BONAPARTE) (1769–1821)

[Journalists] see a great deal of the world.
Our obligation is to pass [what we see] on to others.
MARGARET BOURKE-WHITE (1906–1971)

When a dog bites a man that is not news,
but when a man bites a dog that is news.
CHARLES A. DANA (1819–1897)

[Television] is a medium of entertainment
that permits millions of people to listen to the same joke
at the same time, and yet remain lonesome.
T.S. ELIOT (1888–1965)

This is the first rough draft of history.
PHILIP GRAHAM (1915–1963)

The hand that rules the press, the radio, the screen,
and the far-spread magazine rules the country.
LEARNED HAND (1872–1961)

No news is better than evil news.
(Over time became the proverb "No news is good news")
JAMES I (1566–1625)

Our liberty depends upon the freedom of the press,
and that cannot be limited without being lost.
THOMAS JEFFERSON (1743–1826)

Where there is great power, there is great responsibility.
This is true for broadcasters just as it is for presidents.
LYNDON JOHNSON (1908–1973)

I must say I find television very educational. The minute
somebody turns it on, I go the library and read a good book.
GROUCHO MARX (1886–1961)

The medium is the message.
*Meaning: The form of communication you use to send
a message cannot be separated from the message itself.*
MARSHALL McLUHAN (1911–1980)

A good newspaper, I suppose, is a nation talking to itself.
ARTHUR MILLER (B. 1915)

Good television does what a good book does—
spurs the imagination.
BILL MOYERS (B. 1921)

All I know is just what I read in the papers.
WILL ROGERS (1879–1935)

OLD AGE

The older I get, the greater power I seem to have
to help the world. I am like a snowball—
the further I am rolled the more I gain.
SUSAN B. ANTHONY (1820–1906)

Do not dishonor the old: we shall all be numbered among them.
BIBLE: ECCLESIASTICS 8:7

Grow old along with me!
The best is yet to be.
ROBERT BROWNING (1812–1889)

The man who works and is not bored is never old.
PABLO CASALS (1876–1973)

Eyes that see do not grow old.
COSTA RICAN PROVERB

Eyes of youth have sharp sight,
but commonly not so deep as those of elder age.
ELIZABETH I (1533–1603)

Old soldiers never die,
They simply fade away.
(General MacArthur quoted this song
when dismissed by President Truman)
J. FOLEY (1905–1970)

Old age is...strength and survivorship, triumph over
all kinds of...disappointments, trials and illnesses.
MAGGIE KUHN (1905–1995)

Men are like wine. Some turn to vinegar,
but the best improve with age.
POPE JOHN XXIII (1881–1963)

When one has reached eighty-one, one likes to sit back and
let the world turn by itself, without trying to push it.
SEAN O'CASEY (1880–1964)

Age is a question of mind over matter.
If you don't mind, it doesn't matter.
SATCHEL PAIGE (C. 1906–1982)

Every man desires to live long, but no man would be old.
JONATHAN SWIFT (1667–1745)

My eyes have seen much, but they are not weary.
My ears have heard much, but they thirst for more.
RABINDRANATH TAGORE (1861–1941)

Do not go gentle into that good night,
Old age should burn and rave at close of day;
Rage, rage against the dying of the light.
DYLAN THOMAS (1914–1953)

PEACE

When a king has good counselors, his reign is peaceful.
ASHANTI PROVERB

Blessed are the peacemakers:
for they shall be called the children of God.
BIBLE: MATTHEW 5:3

No problem of human relations is ever insoluble.
RALPH BUNCHE (1904–1971)

You cannot shake hands with a clenched fist.
INDIRA GANDHI (1917–1984)

Means are not to be distinguished from the end.
If violent means are used, there will be bad results.
MOHANDAS GANDHI (1869–1948)

Peace is much more precious than a piece of land.
ANWAR AL-SADAT (1918–1981)

I want peace and I'm willing to fight for it.
HARRY S TRUMAN (1884–1972)

Stability and peace in our land
will not come from the barrel of a gun,
because peace without justice is an impossibility.
DESMOND TUTU (B. 1931)

To be prepared for war is the most
effectual means of preserving peace.
GEORGE WASHINGTON (1732–1799)

We have not yet brought peace to Northern Ireland.
We have created a climate for peace to be respectable.
(On winning the 1976 Nobel Peace Prize
for her efforts to end violence in Northern Ireland)
BETTY WILLIAMS (B. 1943)

Only a peace between equals can last.
WOODROW WILSON (1856–1924)

We do not want the peace of the slave or the peace of the grave.
EMILIANO ZAPATA (C. 1877–1919)

PREJUDICE

The color of the skin is in no way connected with
strength of the mind or intellectual powers.
BENJAMIN BANNEKER (1731–1806)

[We must] see ourselves reflected in every other
human being and . . . respect and honor our differences.
MELBA PATTILLO BEALS (B. 1943)

Prejudices . . . are the most difficult to eradicate from the heart
whose soil has never been loosened or fertilized by education.
CHARLOTTE BRONTË (1816–1855)

We hate some persons because we do not know them,
and will not know them because we hate them.
CHARLES CALEB COLTON (1780–1832)

Prejudice is the child of ignorance.
WILLIAM HAZLITT (1778–1830)

Our lives on this planet are too short,
and the work to be done too great to let the violence of
hate, despair and indifference dominate the land.
ROBERT KENNEDY (1925–1968)

It is better to continue to try to teach or live equality and love
than it would be to have hatred and prejudice.
ROSA PARKS (B. 1913)

Pride of race is an antidote to prejudice.
ARTHUR A. SCHOMBERG (1874–1938)

[Some] men seem to have difficulty in realizing
that people who live differently from themselves still might be
traveling the upward and progressive road of life.
LUTHER STANDING BEAR (1868–1939)

The flour merchant, the housebuilder, and the postman
charge us no less on account of our sex; but when we endeavor to
earn money to pay all these, then indeed we find the difference.
LUCY STONE (1818–1893)

It is never too late to give up our prejudices.
HENRY DAVID THOREAU (1817–1862)

Excellence is the best deterrent to racism or sexism.
OPRAH WINFREY (B. 1954)

PROBLEMS AND SOLUTIONS

One day at a time.
ALCOHOLICS ANONYMOUS MOTTO

For every problem under the sun
There is a remedy, or there's none.
If there's one then go and find it,
And if not then never mind it.
ANONYMOUS

The best laid schemes o' mice and men
Gang aft a-gley.
(often go awry)
ROBERT BURNS (1759–1796)

I don't think necessity is the mother of invention—
invention, in my opinion, arises directly from idleness,
possibly also from laziness. To save oneself trouble.
AGATHA CHRISTIE (1890–1976)

A stitch in time saves nine.
ENGLISH PROVERB

Most people spend more time and energy
going around problems than in trying to solve them.
HENRY FORD (1863–1947)

We will either find a way, or make one.
HANNIBAL (247–183 B.C.)

Strategy is better than strength.
HAUSA PROVERB

Where there's a will there's a way.
GEORGE HERBERT (1593–1633)

Two heads are better than one.
JOHN HEYWOOD (C. 1497–C. 1580)

From the beginning, disability taught
that life could be reinvented.
In fact such an outlook was required.
JOHN HOCKENBERRY (B. 1956)

If you can't go over, go under.
JEWISH PROVERB

Don't cross the bridge till you come to it,
Is a proverb old and of excellent wit.
HENRY WADSWORTH LONGFELLOW (1807–1882)

You can't unscramble eggs.
JOHN PIERPONT MORGAN (1837–1913)

If anything can go wrong, it will.
MURPHY'S LAW (C. 1949)

There is no road so smooth that it has no rough spots.
PANAMANIAN PROVERB

The true creator is necessity who is the mother of our invention.
PLATO (C. 428–348 B.C.)

RESPONSIBILITY

The woods are lovely, dark and deep.
But I have promises to keep,
And miles to go before I sleep,
And miles to go before I sleep.
(from "Stopping by Woods on a Snowy Evening," 1923)
ROBERT FROST (1874–1963)

Nobility has its obligations.
Noblesse oblige.
DUC DE LÉVIS (1764–1830)

Every generation has the obligation to
free men's minds for a look to new worlds.
ELLISON ONIZUKA (1946–1986)

The buck stops here.
This saying began when poker players used a marker called
a "buck" to show which player would take the responsibility
for dealing the cards. This expression was popularized by
the president when he displayed it on a sign on his desk.
HARRY S TRUMAN (1884–1972)

ELEANOR ROOSEVELT: A FIRST LADY WHO TOOK ON NEW RESPONSIBILITIES

When her husband Franklin became president in 1932, Eleanor Roosevelt made it clear she would not limit her role to being a hostess at dinners and tea parties. The United States and the world faced terrible problems: joblessness, hunger, and approaching war. Eleanor Roosevelt traveled to find out about people's problems firsthand. While searching for solutions, she spoke out in her own newspaper column and gave public lectures. After her husband's death, she took on new responsibilites, working with the United Nations to protect human rights. Here are some of her ideas about responsibility:

Remember always that you have not only the right to be an individual, you have an obligation to be one.

We must want for others, not ourselves alone.

I have often thought that less is expected of the president of a great corporation than of an American wife.

Curiously enough, it is often the people who refuse to assume any responsibility who are apt to be the sharpest critics of those who do.

RIGHT AND WRONG

Crime does not pay.
AMERICAN PROVERB

What is wrong today won't be right tomorrow.
DUTCH PROVERB

Two wrongs do not make a right.
ENGLISH PROVERB

The time is always ripe for doing right.
MARTIN LUTHER KING, JR. (1929–1968)

Everybody has an instinctive desire
to do good things and avoid evil.
THOMAS MERTON (1915–1969)

If the first woman that God ever made was strong enough
to turn the world upside down all alone, these women
ought to be able to turn it back and get it right side up.
SOJOURNER TRUTH (C. 1797–1883)

Always do right.
This will gratify some people and astonish the rest.
MARK TWAIN (1835–1910)

THE GOLDEN RULE

The Golden Rule tells people to treat others as they wish to be treated themselves. It has been stated in many ways by religous leaders and philosophers in many times and places. Here are some examples:

We should behave to our friends as
we would wish our friends to behave to us.
ARISTOTLE (384–322 B.C.)

Therefore all things whosoever ye would that men should do to you, do ye even unto them: for this is the law and the prophets.
BIBLE: MATTHEW 7:12

Treat others with justice and respect.
How you treat others will be how they treat you.
BUDDHA (C. 563–483 C. B.C.)

What you do not want done to yourself, do not do to others.
CONFUCIUS (551–479 B.C.)

What is hateful to you do not do to your neighbor.
That is the whole Torah. The rest is commentary.
HILLEL (FL. 30 B.C.–A.D. 10)

No man is a true believer unless he desireth for his brother that which he desireth for himself.
MUHAMMAD (C. 570–632)

SCIENCE AND TECHNOLOGY

An expert is a man who has made all the mistakes
which can be made in a very narrow field.
NIELS BOHR (1885–1962)

I know of nothing more inspiring than that of
making discoveries for one's self.
GEORGE WASHINGTON CARVER (C. 1864–1943)

I was taught that the way of [scientific]
progress is neither swift nor easy.
MARIE CURIE (1867–1934)

I have called this principle, by which each slight variation,
if useful, is preserved, by the term Natural Selection.
CHARLES DARWIN (1809–1882)

We haven't failed. We now know a thousand things
that won't work, so we are much closer to finding what will.
(After a series of experiments that did not yield the solution)
THOMAS EDISON (1847–1931)

I think for months and years. Ninety-nine times,
the conclusion is false. The hundredth time I am right.
ALBERT EINSTEIN (1879–1955)

Steam is no stronger now than it was
a hundred years ago but it is put to better use.
(On the steam engine)
RALPH WALDO EMERSON (1803–1882)

Software is a combination of artistry and engineering . . .
it's like a part of yourself that you have put together.
WILLIAM GATES III (B. 1955)

One machine can do the work of fifty ordinary men.
No machine can do the work of one extraordinary man.
ELBERT HUBBARD (1856–1915)

I was never mechanically minded at making things.
I was mechanically minded in thinking them up.
BEATRICE KENNER (B. 1912)

There is no result in nature without a cause.
Understand the cause and you will have no need to experiment.
LEONARDO DA VINCI (1452–1519)

The scientific mind does not so much provide the
right answers as ask the right questions.
CLAUDE LÉVI-STRAUSS (B. 1908)

Physics is puzzle-solving . . . puzzles created
by nature, not by the mind of man.
MARIA GOEPPERT MAYER (1906–1972)

To every action there is always an equal and opposite reaction.
ISAAC NEWTON (1642–1727)

Chance favors only the prepared mind.
LOUIS PASTEUR (1822–1895)

People don't want technology,
they want solutions to problems.
WANG AN (1920–1990)

I think it was mainly due to the fact that
human flight was generally looked upon
as an impossibility...that scarcely anyone believed it
until he actually saw it with his own eyes.
ORVILLE WRIGHT (1871–1948)

EUREKA! ARCHIMEDES MAKES A DISCOVERY

When the Greek mathematician Archimedes (c. 287–212 B.C.) ran through the streets crying "Eureka!," he was using a common expression of his time. However, he is remembered for this exclamation because he uttered it upon making an important discovery—and because of how he reacted when he made this discovery.

A king had asked Archimedes to find out whether or not his new crown was made of pure gold without melting the crown or harming it in any way. The king had given a jeweler a lump of pure gold to make the crown, but now the king thought that the jeweler might have cheated and used some metal that was less valuable. While he was taking a bath, Archimedes thought of a way to solve the king's problem. According to the historian Plutarch, Archimedes was so excited to have solved this problem that he leapt from the tub and ran out of the bathhouse and into the street (without his clothes), crying "Eureka!" over and over again.

What did Archimedes discover when he used this new method to weigh the crown? Another cheaper metal had been combined with gold to make the crown. Archimedes was able to prove this because the crown displaced more water than the lump of gold. The king had been cheated, but thanks to Archimedes it would never happen again.

SELF-KNOWLEDGE AND SELF-RESPECT

The price of your hat isn't the measure of your brain.
AFRICAN-AMERICAN SAYING

Oh wad some power the giftie gie us
To see oursels as ithers see us!
ROBERT BURNS (1759–1796)

Trust thyself, every heart vibrates to that iron string.
RALPH WALDO EMERSON (1803–1882)

Deal with yourself as an individual worthy of respect,
and make everyone else deal with you the same way.
NIKKI GIOVANNI (B. 1943)

La Raza!
Mejicano!,
Espanol!
Latino
Hispano!
Chicano!
or whatever I call myself,
I look the same
I feel the same
I cry
and
Sing the same
(from I Am Joaquin*)*
RODOLFO "CORKY" GONZALES (B. 1928)

I cannot and will not cut my conscience to fit this year's fashions.
LILLIAN HELLMAN (1905–1984)

If I am not for myself, who will be for me?
But if I am for myself only, what am I? And if not now, when?
HILLEL (FL. 30 B.C.–A.D. 10)

Life can only be understood backwards,
but it must be lived forwards.
SÖREN KIERKEGAARD (1813–1855)

I don't know who my grandfather was;
I am much more concerned to know what his grandson will be.
ABRAHAM LINCOLN (1809–1865)

Do not measure another person's coat by how well it fits your body.
MALAY PROVERB

No woman should say, "I am but a woman!"
But a woman! What more can you ask to be?
MARIA MITCHELL (1818–1889)

The way I was taught, being black was a plus, always.
Being a human being, being in America, and being black,
all three were the greatest things that could happen to you.
The combination was unbeatable.
LEONTYNE PRICE (B. 1927)

All men seek esteem, the best by lifting themselves, which is hard
to do. The rest by showing up others, which is much easier.
MARY RENAULT (1905–1983)

No one can make you feel inferior without your consent.
ELEANOR ROOSEVELT (1884–1962)

The important thing is not what
they think of me, it is what I think of them.
VICTORIA (1819–1901)

SPORTS

You can't win unless you know how to lose.
KAREEM ABDUL-JABBAR (B. 1947)

Float like a butterfly, sting like a bee.
*(describing his technique as a boxer; Ali avoided
his opponents by gracefully "floating" beyond their reach,
and then delivering sharp "stinging" punches)*
MUHAMMAD ALI (B. 1942)

Baseball has been known in the Northern States as far back as the memory of the oldest inhabitant reacheth, and must be regarded as the national pastime, the same as cricket is for the British.
ANONYMOUS

Those who play the game do not see it as clearly as those who watch.
CHINESE PROVERB

I believe that football, perhaps more than any other sport,
tends to instill in men the feeling that victory comes
through hard, slavish team play, self-confidence,
and enthusiasm that amounts to dedication.
DWIGHT D. EISENHOWER (1890–1969)

Statistically 100% of the shots you don't take don't go in.
WAYNE GRETSKY (B. 1961)

Talent wins games, but teamwork and
intelligence win championships.
MICHAEL JORDAN (B. 1963)

Winning isn't everything, but wanting to win is.
*(misquoted by sportswriter Red Saunders, it became the popular saying,
"Winning isn't everything—it is the only thing.")*
VINCE LOMBARDI (1913–1970)

Football isn't a contact sport, it's a collision sport.
VINCE LOMBARDI (1913–1970)

Great champions...are those who are driven to show the world—
and prove to themselves—just how good they are.
NANCY LOPEZ (B. 1957)

Sports [teach you that] it is good to compete,
good to run, good to sweat, good to get dirty,
good to feel tired and healthy, and refreshed.
MARTINA NAVRATILOVA (B. 1956)

Nothing to mountaineering, just a little physical endurance,
a good deal of brains, lots of practice, and plenty of warm clothing.
ANNIE SMITH PECK (1850–1935)

When the One Great Scorer comes to
write against your name—
He marks—not that you won or lost—
but how you played the game.
(Over time this verse became the proverb,
"It's not whether you win or lose but how you play the game.")
GRANTLAND RICE (1880–1954)

Every inning is a new adventure in baseball.
JACKIE ROBINSON (1919–1972)

Never let the fear of striking out get in your way.
"BABE" RUTH (1895–1948)

YOGI BERRA COMMENTS ON BASEBALL AND LIFE

When Lawrence Peter (Yogi) Berra (b. 1925) made it to the major leagues, he found out that he was expected to talk to reporters as well as play ball. Berra didn't fit the handsome, poised image they had of an athlete. Reporters and fans laughed at him, but he laughed, too. Soon people saw that Yogi was quite a ballplayer. He played in 10 World Series and was elected to the Baseball Hall of Fame. People also began to look forward to hearing his "Yogisms." His unique logic, as illustrated below, made whatever he said memorable.

It ain't over till its over.

Baseball is 90 percent mental.
The other half is physical.

You can observe a lot by watching.

Anybody who is popular
is bound to be disliked.

Nobody ever goes there anymore.
It's too crowded.

SUCCESS

Success has many parents, but failure is an orphan.
*Meaning: Many people are willing to take credit for a successful
effort, but no one is willing to take responsibility for failure.*
AMERICAN PROVERB

You may encounter many defeats,
but you must not be defeated.
MAYA ANGELOU (B. 1928)

If at first you don't succeed,
try, try again.
ANONYMOUS

I don't know the key to success,
but the key to failure is trying to please everybody.
BILL COSBY (B. 1937)

Success is counted sweetest
By those who ne'er succeed.
EMILY DICKINSON (1830–1886)

Nothing succeeds like success.
ALEXANDRE DUMAS (1802–1870)

If A is a success in life, then A equals x plus y plus z.
Work is x; y is play and z is keeping your mouth shut.
ALBERT EINSTEIN (1879–1955)

Any man who is prepared for defeat would be
half defeated before he commenced. I hope for success; shall do
all in my power to secure it, and trust in God for the rest.
DAVID G. FARRAGUT (1801–1870)

Little strokes
Fell great oaks.
BENJAMIN FRANKLIN (1706–1790)

Trifles make perfection, but perfection is no trifle.
ITALIAN PROVERB

Fall seven times, stand up eight.
JAPANESE PROVERB

All things come round to him who will but wait.
HENRY WADSWORTH LONGFELLOW (1807–1882)

I do not know anyone who has gotten to the top
without hard work. . . . It will not always
get you to the top, but should get you pretty near.
MARGARET THATCHER (B. 1925)

All you need in life is ignorance and confidence,
and then success is sure.
MARK TWAIN (1835–1910)

We are not interested in the possibilities of defeat.
VICTORIA (1819–1901)

There is always room at the top.
DANIEL WEBSTER (1782–1852)

TIME

As long as the moon shall rise,
As long as the river shall flow,
As long as the sun shall shine,
As long as the grass shall grow.
These words were used in nineteenth-century treaties
made between the United States Government
and American Indian nations.
ANONYMOUS

To every thing there is a season,
and a time to every purpose under heaven;
A time to be born, and a time to die; a time to plant,
and a time to pluck up that which is planted.
BIBLE: ECCLESIASTES 3:1–2

Time and tide wait for no man.
WILLIAM BRADFORD (1590–1657)

It is astonishing how short a time it takes
for something wonderful to happen.
FRANCES BURNETT (1849–1924)

Here today, gone tomorrow.
JOHN CALVIN (1509–1564)

Time heals all wounds.
GEOFFREY CHAUCER (C. 1343–1400)

I recommend that you take care of minutes;
for hours will take care of themselves.
LORD CHESTERFIELD (1694–1773)

Life is short, and it's up to you to make it sweet.
SADIE DELANY (B. 1889)

Never leave that till tomorrow which you can do today.
BENJAMIN FRANKLIN (1706–1790)

Take time for all things. Great haste makes great waste.
BENJAMIN FRANKLIN (1706–1790)

Procrastination is the thief of time.
ALEXANDER HAMILTON (1755–1804)

Respect the past . . . but do not make the mistake of confusing it
with the present nor seek in it the ideals of the future.
JOSÉ INGENIEROS (1877–1925)

One moment of time is more valuable
than a thousand pieces of gold.
KOREAN PROVERB

Time flies.
(tempis fugit)
LATIN PROVERB

If we want to work out a policy for the present,
we must examine the past and prepare for the future.
LIVY (59 B.C.–A.D. 17)

Better late than never.
LU HSÜN (1881–1936)

Time is a sort of river of passing events, and strong
is its current; no sooner is a thing brought to sight
than it is swept by and another takes its place.
MARCUS AURELIUS (121–180 A.D.)

Half of our life is spent trying to find something to do
with the time we have rushed through life to save.
WILL ROGERS (1879–1935)

Ah! The clock is always slow!
It is later than you think!
ROBERT SERVICE (1874–1958)

The same thing happened today that
happened yesterday, only to different people.
WALTER WINCHELL (1897–1972)

TRAVEL AND ADVENTURE

He who does not travel will not know the value of men.
ALGERIAN PROVERB

That's one small step for [a] man, one giant leap for mankind.
(upon taking his first steps on the moon, July 20, 1969)
NEIL ARMSTRONG (B. 1930)

You've got to be careful if you don't know
where you are going, because you may not get there.
YOGI BERRA (B. 1925)

Seeing Earth from 170 miles out in space
is not like standing on Earth and looking at the moon.
GUION BLUFORD (B. 1942)

Men travel faster now, but I do not know if they go to better things.
WILLA CATHER (1873–1947)

[I] had ambition not only to go farther than any man
had ever been before, but as far as it was possible for a man to go.
JAMES COOK (1728–1779)

The true adventurer goes forth aimless and
uncalculating to meet and greet unknown fate.
O. HENRY (1862–1910)

He travels the fastest who travels alone.
RUDYARD KIPLING (1865–1936)

Travelers are always discoverers, especially those
who travel by air. There are no signposts on the sky
to show a man has passed that way before.
ANNE MORROW LINDBERGH (B. 1906)

We travel to learn. I have never been in any country
where they do not do something better than we do it.
MARIA MITCHELL (1818–1889)

The bicycle is the most civilized conveyance known to man.
Other forms of transport grow daily more nightmarish.
Only the bicycle remains pure at heart.
IRIS MURDOCH (B. 1919)

I went to the woods because I wished to live deliberately,
to front only the essential facts of life,
and see if I could not learn what it had to teach.
HENRY DAVID THOREAU (1817–1862)

I got more thrill out of flying before I had ever
been in the air at all—while lying in bed
thinking how exciting it would be to fly.
ORVILLE WRIGHT (1871–1948)

TRUTH AND REALITY

Liars, even when they speak the truth, are not believed.
ARISTOTLE (384–322 B.C.)

Always tell the truth in the form of a joke.
ARMENIAN PROVERB

The truth shall make you free.
BIBLE: JOHN 8:32

A truth that's told with bad intent
Beats all the lies you can invent.
WILLIAM BLAKE (1757–1827)

Honesty is the best policy.
MIGUEL DE CERVANTES (1547–1616)

Truth may be stretched but cannot be broken.
It always gets above falsehood as oil does above water.
MIGUEL DE CERVANTES (1547–1616)

The simple is the seal of the true,
and beauty is the splendor of truth.
SUBRAHMANYAN CHANDRASEKHAR (1910–1995)

Tell all the truth, but tell it slant—
The truth must dazzle gradually—
Or every man be blind.
EMILY DICKINSON (1830–1886)

Truth is proper and beautiful at all times and in all places.
FREDERICK DOUGLASS (1817–1895)

When you have eliminated the impossible, whatever remains,
however improbable, must be the truth.
(Sherlock Holmes to Watson in The Sign of Four*)*
ARTHUR CONAN DOYLE (1859–1930)

Truth is what stands the test of experience.
ALBERT EINSTEIN (1879–1955)

An exaggeration is a truth that has lost its temper.
KAHLIL GIBRAN (1883–1931)

If now isn't a good time for the truth,
I don't see when we'll get to it.
NIKKI GIOVANNI (B. 1943)

The truth isn't always beautiful, but the hunger for it is.
NADINE GORDIMER (B. 1923)

It does not require many words to speak the truth.
CHIEF JOSEPH (HINMATON-YALAKTIT) (C. 1840–1904)

It is true that you may fool all of the people some of the time;
you can even fool some of the people all of the time;
but you can't fool all of the people all of the time.
ABRAHAM LINCOLN (1809–1865)

Believe only half of what you see and nothing you hear.
EDGAR ALLAN POE (1809–1849)

Oh, what a tangled web we weave
When first we practice to deceive!
SIR WALTER SCOTT (1771–1832)

Things happen in life so fantastic that
no imagination could have invented them.
ISAAC BASHEVIS SINGER (1904–1991)

It takes two to speak the truth—one to speak and another to hear.
HENRY DAVID THOREAU (1817–1862)

When in doubt, tell the truth.
MARK TWAIN (1835–1910)

Falsehoods not only disagree with truths,
but usually quarrel among themselves.
DANIEL WEBSTER (1782–1852)

There is nothing as powerful as truth—
and often nothing so strange.
DANIEL WEBSTER (1782–1852)

SOJOURNER TRUTH SPEAKS WITH HONESTY AND PURPOSE

Born into slavery, an uneducated woman in New York became one of the best known advocates for the rights of African-Americans and women. Her slave name had been Isabella, but she changed her name to reflect her new life and her new goals. Sojourner Truth (c. 1797–1883) sojourned, or traveled, across the country to share a basic truth: All people deserve equal rights and opportunities. She was tall and strong and she captivated audiences with her deep voice, quick wit, and knowledge of the Bible. She also used examples from her own life to impress people with the strength of women and the injustices of slavery. In 1850, she was the only African-American woman to speak at the Ohio Women's Rights Convention. In her speech, she repeated the question, "And ain't I woman?" over and over again, using the question to illustrate that she had shown that she had as much strength, endurance, and courage as any man when she worked in the fields, faced physical punishment, and watched her children sold away into slavery.

After slavery was abolished, Sojourner traveled on, still speaking the truth. She campaigned for more rights for African-Americans and for women's right to vote, but she did not live to see these goals become a reality. Here are some of the things she said:

That man over there says that women need to be helped
into carriages. . . . And to have the best place everywhere.
Nobody ever helps me into carriages. . . . Or gives me
the best place! And ain't I a woman? . . . I have plowed and
planted and gathered into barns and no man could head me!
And ain't I a woman? I could work as much as a man . . .
And ain't I a woman?

I . . . can't read a book, but I can read the people.

Truth burns up error.

WAYS TO SAY: YOU CANNOT ALWAYS BELIEVE WHAT YOU SEE

Appearances may be deceiving.
AESOP (FL. C. 500 B.C.)

Cold hands, warm heart.
AMERICAN PROVERB

The teeth are smiling, but is the heart?
CONGO PROVERB

The eyes see only what the mind is prepared to comprehend.
ROBERTSON DAVIES (1913–1995)

Don't judge a book by its cover.
ENGLISH PROVERB

Things are seldom what they seem
Skimmed milk oft masquerades as cream.
SIR W. S. GILBERT (1836–1911)

All that glisters is not gold.
(Now more commonly quoted as the proverb
"All that glitters is not gold")
WILLIAM SHAKESPEARE (1564–1616)

WAR

I must study politics and war that my sons
may have liberty to study mathematics and philosophy.
JOHN ADAMS (1735–1826)

It is wise statesmanship which suggests
in time of peace we must prepare for war.
CLARA BARTON (1821–1912)

A revolution is an opinion backed by bayonets.
NAPOLEON I (NAPOLEON BONAPARTE) (1769–1821)

War is a series of catastrophes which results in victory.
GEORGES CLEMENCEAU (1841–1929)

There never was a good war or a bad peace.
BENJAMIN FRANKLIN (1706–1790)

The battle, sir, is not to the strong alone;
it is to the vigilant, the active, and the brave.
PATRICK HENRY (1736–1799)

Guns, bombs, rockets and warships are all symbols
of human failure. They are necessary symbols. They protect
what we cherish. But they are witness to human folly.
LYNDON B. JOHNSON (1908–1973)

It is well that war is so terrible, or we should grow too fond of it.
ROBERT E. LEE (1807–1870)

War is not just a victory or loss.... People die.
MAYA LIN (B. 1959)

In war there is no substitute for victory.
GENERAL DOUGLAS MACARTHUR (1880–1964)

Divide and conquer.
NICCOLÒ MACHIAVELLI (1469–1527)

[In times of war] He who overcomes an enemy by fraud
is as much to be praised as he who overcomes him by force.
NICCOLÓ MACHIAVELLI (1469–1527)

You can no more win a war than you can win an earthquake.
JEANETTE RANKIN (1880–1973)

The right of conquest has no foundation
other than the right of the strongest.
JEAN JACQUES ROUSSEAU (1712–1778)

Sometime they'll give a war and nobody will come.
CARL SANDBURG (1878–1967)

When men talk about defense, they always claim
to be protecting the women and children, but they never
ask the women and children what they think.
PATRICIA SCHROEDER (B. 1940)

There is many a boy here today who looks upon war as all glory, but boys, it is all hell. You can bear this warning voice to generations yet to come. I look upon war with horror.
WILLIAM TECUMSEH SHERMAN (1820–1891)

Where they make a desert they call it peace.
TACITUS (C. A.D. 56–C. 120)

Discipline is the soul of the army. It makes small numbers formidable; procures success to the weak, and esteem to all.
GEORGE WASHINGTON (1732–1799)

FIGHTING WORDS: "BEWARE OF GREEKS BEARING GIFTS" AND MORE

In every war, slogans and literature served as reminders of what people were fighting for and were used to glorify those who fought for the cause. However, some often-quoted words of war may make little sense today, without explanations like the ones below to help you understand what these words mean.

Don't fire until you see the whites of their eyes!
AMERICAN COLONIAL LEADER (1775)
Meaning: Don't shoot until the enemy is close, otherwise you will waste ammunition. This command was first uttered at the Battle of Bunker Hill, June 17, 1775 by Colonel William Prescott or General Israel Putnam. The Americans knew that the British had more troops and more ammunition, but they were determined to hold the hill as long as they could. The British won the battle, but it cost them many lives. The

Americans also suffered many casualties, but this slogan reminded everyone of the determination and courage of the Colonial militia.

Beware of Greeks bearing gifts.

ENGLISH PROVERB

Meaning: Never trust an enemy—even when the enemy appears to be doing something nice. This English proverb comes from an ancient legend that tells how the great city of Troy and most of its people were destroyed when their enemies, the Greeks, pretended to want an end to the war they were fighting. They presented the Trojans with a huge wooden horse as a peace offering. The Trojans pulled the horse through the gates of their walled city. Later, while the Trojans slept, Greek soldiers who had been hiding inside the horse crept out and opened the gate for the many warriors waiting outside.

I have nothing to offer but blood, toil, tears, and sweat.

WINSTON CHURCHILL (1874–1965)

Meaning: I will give everything I have to protect and preserve my country. When Churchill was elected prime minister in 1940, he spoke to the House of Commons and to his nation to prepare them for the continued hardships of World War II and to inspire them to believe they had the strength and the determination to withstand and defeat their enemy.

Remember the Alamo!

TEXAS REBEL SOLDIERS (1836)

Meaning: Remember the rebels who died defending the Alamo mission A small, determined group of Anglo, Mexican, and African-American rebels fought a large army of Mexican soldiers during a surprise attack. When the battle was over, more than 180 of the rebels had been killed, including Davy Crockett and Jim Bowie, who had come to Texas especially to help the rebel cause. Texans and Americans were so outraged at this attack that they rushed to join the rebel army. The expanded rebel forces, using "Remember the Alamo!" as their battle cry, charged after the Mexican Army and drove them out of Texas. Within months, Texas won its independence from Mexico.

Theirs not to reason why,
Theirs but to do and die.
ALFRED, LORD TENNYSON (1809–1892)
Meaning: They are so loyal they will not question their orders, even if it puts their lives in danger. Tennyson wrote his poem "The Charge of the Light Brigade" in 1854, after reading a newspaper account about British soldiers during the Crimean War who got the wrong orders by mistake and then unhesitatingly rode off to face Russian troops they knew they could not defeat. For Tennyson, this event symbolized patriotism and courage, but for many people today it is a reminder that there are times when people should not blindly follow orders.

WEALTH AND POVERTY

Money speaks sense in a language all nations understand.
APHRA BEHN (1640–1689)

Wealth maketh many friends.
BIBLE: PROVERBS 19:4

The love of money is the root of all evil.
BIBLE: I TIMOTHY 6:10

I have always known that being very poor, which we were,
had nothing to do with lovingness or familyness,
or character or any of that. . . . We were quite clear that
what we didn't have didn't have anything to do
with what we were.
LUCILLE CLIFTON (B. 1936)

Annual income twenty pounds, annual expenditure
nineteen six, result happiness. Annual income twenty pounds,
annual expenditures twenty ought and six, result misery.
CHARLES DICKENS (1812–1870)

A penny saved is a penny earned.
ENGLISH PROVERB

Money helps, though not so much
as you think when you don't have it.
LOUISE ERDRICH (B. 1954)

Light purse, heavy heart.
BENJAMIN FRANKLIN (1706–1790)

The malady which brings the greatest distress
to mankind—to even the wisest and the cleverest of us—
is the plague of poverty.
IHARA SAIKAKU (1642–1693)

I complained that I had no shoes
until I met a man who had no feet.
PERSIAN PROVERB

Poverty is a pain but not a disgrace.
SCOTTISH PROVERB

A rich child often sits in a poor mother's lap.
SPANISH PROVERB

The man is the richest whose pleasures are the cheapest.
HENRY DAVID THOREAU (1817–1862)

WISDOM

We need to haunt the halls of history
and listen anew to the ancestors' wisdom.
MAYA ANGELOU (B. 1928)

Wisdom is not acquired without investigation.
SANKARA ARCHARGA (C. 769–820)

The value of wisdom is above rubies.
BIBLE: JOB 28:18

So teach us to number our days,
that we may apply our hearts unto wisdom.
BIBLE: PSALMS 90:12

A wise man adapts himself to circumstances,
as water shapes itself to the vessel that holds it.
CHINESE PROVERB

All human wisdom is summed up
in two words, wait and hope.
ALEXANDRE DUMAS (1802–1870)

Genius has many limitations,
but stupidity is not thus handicapped.
ELBERT HUBBARD (1856–1915)

A single conversation . . . with a wise man
is better than ten years mere study of books.
HENRY WADSWORTH LONGFELLOW (1807–1882)

Nine-tenths of wisdom consists of being wise in time.
THEODORE ROOSEVELT (1858–1919)

WORK

The shoemaker makes a good shoe because he makes nothing else.
RALPH WALDO EMERSON (1803–1882)

Many hands make light work.
ENGLISH PROVERB

My grandfather once told me that there were two kinds of people:
those who do the work and those who take the credit. He told me to
try to be in the first group: there was much less competition.
INDIRA GANDHI (1917–1984)

Labor disgraces no man. Unfortunately,
you occasionally find men who disgrace labor.
ULYSSES S. GRANT (1822–1885)

All work and no play makes Jack a dull boy.
JAMES HOWELL (c. 1594–1666)

By the work one knows the workman.
JEAN DE LA FONTAINE (1621–1695)

When you are asked if you can do a job, tell 'em,
"Certainly I can." Then get busy and find out how to do it.
THEODORE ROOSEVELT (1858–1919)

When you play, play hard; when you work, don't play at all.
THEODORE ROOSEVELT (1858–1919)

Leave women, then, to find their sphere.
And do not tell us before we are born even that our province is
to cook dinners, darn stockings, and sew on buttons.
LUCY STONE (1818–1893)

Let your guest be a guest for two days,
on the third day give him a hoe!
SWAHILI PROVERB

Work consists of whatever a body is obliged to do, and. . . .
Play consists of whatever a body is not obliged to do.
MARK TWAIN (1835–1910)

WRITING

Writing is nothing more than a guided dream.
JORGE LUIS BORGES (1899–1986)

I am a writer perhaps because I am not a talker.
GWENDOLYN BROOKS (B. 1917)

Writing is like baseball or piano playing.
You have to practice if you want to be successful.
BETSY BYARS (B. 1928)

For me the pleasure of writing comes from inventing stories.
ROALD DAHL (1916–1990)

Poetry is as exact a science as geometry.
GUSTAVE FLAUBERT (1821–1880)

For the writer, there is nothing quite like having someone say
that he or she understands, that you have reached them
and affected them with what you have written.
VIRGINIA HAMILTON (B. 1936)

Write what you like; there is no other rule.
O. HENRY (1862–1910)

Anyone may be an honorable man and yet write verse badly.
MOLIÈRE (1622–1673)

The point of good writing is knowing when to stop.
LUCY MAUD MONTGOMERY (1874–1942)

You don't have to fight dragons to write books.
You just have to live deeply the life you've been given.
KATHERINE PATERSON (B. 1932)

The wastebasket is a writer's best friend.
ISAAC BASHEVIS SINGER (1904–1991)

It is wise to write on many subjects, to try many topics
so that you may find the right and inspiring one.
HENRY DAVID THOREAU (1817–1862)

YOUTH

Boys will be boys.
AMERICAN PROVERB

Even a child is known by his doings.
BIBLE: PROVERBS 20:11

It is the responsibility of every adult—especially parents,
educators, and religious leaders—to make sure that children hear
what we have learned from the lessons of life, and to hear
over and over that we love them and that they are not alone.
MARIAN WRIGHT EDELMAN (B. 1939)

You are young, gifted and Black
We must begin to tell our young,
There is a world waiting for you,
Yours is the quest that's just begun.
JAMES WELDON JOHNSON (1871–1938)

A twelve-year-old is starting to find out that he can do
certain things as well as his parents or his teacher.
By the time he's fifteen he probably can do some things better.
GORDON KORMAN (B. 1963)

What its children become, that will the community become.
SUZANNE LA FOLLETTE (1893–1983)

One of the advantages of being very young is that you
don't let the facts get in the way of your imagination.
SAM LEVENSON (1911–1980)

A boy's will is the wind's will,
And the thoughts of youth are long, long thoughts.
HENRY WADSWORTH LONGFELLOW (1807–1882)

American youth attributes much more significance to
arriving at driver's license age than at voting age.
MARSHALL MCLUHAN (1911–1980)

You will be running to the
far corners of the universe; . . .
Run!
Be strong.
For you are the mother of a people.
MESCALERO APACHE SONG

I say to the young:
Do not stop thinking of life as an adventure. You have no security
unless you can live bravely, excitingly, imaginatively.
ELEANOR ROOSEVELT (1884–1962)

Biographical Index

This Index lists all the people quoted in the book, tells briefly about their lives and accomplishments, and indicates under which subject or subjects they are quoted.

When a subject is marked with a **, it means the quotation appears in a special box and additional information about the person or the meaning of the quote is also provided.

Each name is listed in alphabetical order, family name first. Cross references are provided for people who are better known by pen names or stage names than by the names they were given at birth. Figures who are known by their first name and a title (such as James I, King of England or Mother Teresa) are listed under their names, not their titles.

Since some quotations cannot be traced back to a specific person but are attributed to a traditional source of wisdom, such as a religious text like the Bible, or to a proverb or traditional song or saying, these sources are also included within this Index.

ABDUL-JABBAR, KAREEM (B. 1947)
U.S. basketball player known for his hook shot. This 7′2″ star played in the NBA from 1969 to 1989. Named Ferdinand Lewis Alcindor at birth, he changed his name in 1971 after he adopted the Black Muslim faith.
Sports

ACTON, LORD (1834–1902)
British historian who wrote many essays and edited the *Cambridge Modern History*. His full name was John Emerich Edward Dahlberg, Baron Acton.
Government and Politics

ADAMS, ABIGAIL (1744–1818)
American patriot and first lady whose letters to friends and family members reveal her opinions on many issues. Her husband John served as president and her son John Quincy also became president. Friends who sought her opinions included Thomas Jefferson and historian Mercy Otis Warren. Abigail Adams urged the founders of the new United States to grant more rights to women and to abolish slavery.
Character, Education and Learning

ADAMS, ANSEL (1902–1984)
U.S. photographer best known for his dramatic black and white photographs of the West. His photos of mountains, forests, and rivers also inspired people to work for wilderness conservation.
Art

ADAMS, JOHN (1735–1826)
Second president of the United States and one of the key figures in the founding of the new nation. He was born in Massachusetts and became a lawyer. By 1765 he was speaking out against injustices of British rule. Adams was one of the signers of the Declaration of Independence and served as George Washington's vice president before he was elected to the office of president in 1796.
Food, Freedom, War

ADDAMS, JANE (1860–1935)
U.S. human rights worker and one of two winners of the 1931 Nobel Prize for Peace. With Ellen Starr Gates, Addams founded a special community center in Chicago called Hull House. Addams did what she could to improve conditions for the poor. She helped get laws passed that limited child labor and improved working conditions for women and housing for the poor.
Citizenship and Patriotism, Community and City Life, Justice and Equality

ADDISON, JOSEPH (1672–1719)
British essayist and politician remembered for his publication *The Spectator*. Together with his coeditor, Richard Steele, Addison used *The Spectator* to present his views on many subjects, including science, philosophy, love, and proper manners.
Books and Reading, Character, Education and Learning

AESOP (FL. C. 550 B.C.)
Greek storyteller whose fables have been passed down and retold for thousands of years.

Few facts about Aesop's life are known (some modern scholars even doubt he was a real person), but his name means "The Ethiopian" and most accounts say he was a slave until late in his life.

Animals**, Apologies and Excuses, Courage, Effort and Enthusiasm, Helping and Kindness, Human Nature**

ALBRIGHT, MADELINE (B. 1937)

First woman Secretary of State of the United States, appointed by President William Clinton in 1996. Albright was born in Czechoslovakia and came to the U.S. as a child. She served as U.N. ambassador before becoming Secretary of State.

History

ALCOTT, LOUISA MAY (1832–1888)

U.S. author of *Little Women* (1868–1869), a popular novel that tells the story of four sisters growing up in a small New England town during the Civil War era. At an early age, Alcott began to help support her family by working a variety of jobs. During the Civil War she served as a nurse, and later wrote about her experiences in *Hospital Sketches.*

Beauty, Books and Reading, Friendship and Loyalty

ALCOHOLICS ANONYMOUS (A. A.) (FOUNDED 1935)

Worldwide organization of individuals who have had problems caused by drinking; they follow certain steps in a recovery program to change their behavior to end their drinking.

Problems and Solutions

ALI (C. 602–661)

This Islamic writer was also the son-in-law and adopted son of Muhammad, the prophet and founder of the Islamic religion. His full name was Ali ibn Abi Talib.

Friendship and Loyalty

ALI, MUHAMMAD (B. 1942)

U.S. boxing champion who became the first heavyweight to win the championship title four times. Born Cassius Clay, he changed his named when he adopted the Black Muslim religion in 1964. He was known for his playful, confident style; he wrote poems about his own abilities and the weaknesses of his opponents. He also spoke out on issues such as civil rights.

Creativity and Ideas, Sports

ALFONSO X (1221–1284)

King of Castile who was also known as Alfonso the Wise or Learned. He proclaimed a code of laws that became the basis for the Spanish legal system. For hundreds of years Castile was a kingdom; today it is part of Spain.

Confidence

ANAYA, RUDOLFO (B. 1937)

U.S. author and educator, much of whose work celebrates Mexican-American culture. His novel *Bless Me, Ultima* is among his best-known works.

Community and City Life

ANGELOU, MAYA (B. 1928)

U.S. writer, poet, dancer, and actress best known for her autobiographical work *I Know*

Why the Caged Bird Sings, which tells how a young African-American girl survives and blossoms despite many hardships.
Ability and Talent, Home, Success, Wisdom

ANONYMOUS
This word means "without a name" and refers to authors who choose not to sign their names, or to works for which an author is unknown.
Friendship and Loyalty, History, Mathematics, Sports, Time

ANTHONY, SUSAN B. (1820–1906)
U.S. women's rights leader remembered as one of the leaders in the movement to secure women the right to vote.
Justice and Equality, Old Age

ANZALDÚA, GLORIA (B. 1942)
U.S. author known for her poetry, which reveals her strong sense of self and her Tejana heritage.
Change

ARBUS, DIANE (1923–1971)
U.S. photographer known for her startling portraits of all kinds of people.
Art

ARCHARGA, SANKARA (C. 769–820)
Hindu scholar whose writings presented wise sayings and rules to help people live a good life.
Wisdom

ARCHIMEDES (C. 287–212 B.C.)
Sicilian mathematician who also explored problems of physics and engineering. He used levers and pulleys to move heavy objects, including a ship loaded with people and cargo. He also discovered that each object has a center of gravity, the single point at which the force of gravity seems to act on the object.
*Science and Technology**

ARISTOTLE (384–322 B.C.)
Greek philosopher, educator, and scientist who was a student of the great philosopher Plato. Aristotle explored all aspects of human knowledge, and he believed that thought is the tool by which all knowledge is obtained. He wrote many works, including research notes and historical records. His writing presents his views on logic and thought, nature, politics, and literature.
Anger, Education and Learning, Government and Politics, Human Nature, Justice and Equality, Nature, Right and Wrong, Truth and Reality

ARMSTRONG, LOUIS (1901–1971)
U.S. jazz musician known for his brilliant trumpet playing and his gravelly singing voice. As a teenager he played with local bands in New Orleans; by 1928 he was playing with the finest jazz musicians in the nation and was among the best-known African-American recording artists in the world.
Music

ARMSTRONG, NEIL (B. 1930)
U.S. astronaut and the first human being to walk on the moon. He made his first space flight in 1966. On July 20, 1969, he and "Buzz" Aldrin landed the *Apollo 11* lunar module *Eagle* on the moon.
Travel and Adventure

ASHE, ARTHUR (1943–1993)

Tennis star who was the only African-American player to win the Wimbeldon, the Australian Open, and to twice win the U.S. Open men's single title. He also wrote a history of African-American athletes and spoke out on civil rights issues. In 1992 he also began to speak out about AIDS education, revealing that he himself had contracted the disease during heart surgery.
Introduction

ASPCA (AMERICAN SOCIETY FOR THE PREVENTION OF CRUELTY TO ANIMALS)
Animals

ASTAIRE, FRED (1899–1987)

U.S. dancer and film star who often starred in romantic comedies in which he danced his way into the leading lady's heart.
Dance

ASTOR, NANCY (1879–1964)

U.S.-born British politician who in 1919 became the first woman to serve in the British Parliament. She was known for her humor and wit and she often spoke out for the rights of women and children. She also spoke out against drinking and the sale of alcoholic beverages.
Health

ATHENIAN OATH, THE (C. 450 B.C.)

The quotation in this book comes from an oath or promise all young men had to take when they reached the age of seventeen. In the oath, the young men promised never to do anything dishonest or cowardly, to fight for the ideals of Athens, and to obey all its laws.
Citizenship and Patriotism

ATWOOD, MARGARET (B. 1939)

Canadian author who has won acclaim for her novels, poetry, children's books, and short stories.
Books and Reading

AUGUSTINE, SAINT (354–430)

Roman Christian leader who lived most of his life in North Africa. He studied other religious philosophies before becoming a baptized Christian in 387. Three years later he became a priest. In 391 he became bishop of Hippo (in North Africa). His famous books include *Confessions* and *De Civitate Dei*.
Justice and Equality

AUSTEN, JANE (1775–1817)

British author whose novels, including *Pride and Prejudice* and *Sense and Sensibility*, feature strong, determined heroines and are still popular today.
Family, History, Home

BACON, FRANCIS (1561–1626)

British politician, philosopher, and scientist who was one of the earliest supporters of using experiments and observation to learn more about nature. He also served in Parliament and was knighted in 1603.
Ability and Talent, Education and Learning, Faith and Hope, Manners

BALANCHINE, GEORGE (1904–1983)
U.S. dancer and choreographer credited with creating a new style of ballet. He was born in Russia and came to the U.S. in 1933.
Dance

BANNEKER, BENJAMIN (1731–1806)
American Colonial scientist who helped design and plan the city of Washington D. C. In 1796 he became the first African-American to publish his own annual almanac.
Prejudice, Self-Knowledge and Self-Respect

BARNARD, FRED (C. 1927)
U.S. journalist who in the 1920s wrote for an advertising publication called *Printers' Ink*.
News and the Media

BARRIE, J. M. (1860–1937)
British author of *Peter Pan* and 34 other novels and plays. Born in Scotland, he moved to London to pursue a career as a writer. His full name and title was Sir James Matthew Barrie.
Helping and Kindness

BARTON, CLARA (1821–1912)
U.S. nurse and founder of the American Red Cross. During the Civil War, Barton nursed wounded soldiers. In 1869, on a trip to Switzerland, she learned of the International Red Cross and became determined to establish a branch in the U.S.
War

BARZUN, JACQUES (B. 1907)
U.S. educator and historian who specializes in the history of ideas.
Education and Learning

BASHŌ, MATSUO (1644–1694)
Japanese poet known for his haiku, short poems about 14 syllables long. He believed that a poet must observe and understand a subject completely in order to write a poem about it.
Nature

BEALS, MELBA PATTILLO (B. 1943)
U.S. civil rights activist and journalist. As a teenager in 1957, Beals made history by being one of the first nine African-American students to attend Central High School in Little Rock, Arkansas. This event marked the beginning of the end of segregation of students by race in public schools.
Prejudice

BEARD, CHARLES A. (1874–1948)
U.S. historian who wrote more than 70 books on American history and U.S. foreign policy.
Faith and Hope

BEARDEN, ROMARE (1914–1988)
U.S. artist whose collages and paintings explore many aspects of African-American culture.
Nature

BEECHER, HENRY WARD (1813–1887)
U.S. minister and abolitionist known for his clever, dramatic sermons. He was the brother of Harriet Beecher Stowe, whose novel *Uncle Tom's Cabin* also helped advance the abolitionist movement.
Anger, Animals, Language and Words

BEHN, APHRA (1640–1689)

British author who wrote under the pen name Astraea. Behn was very poor and determined to earn money. She became the first woman in England to be a professional writer. She wrote more than 15 plays and several novels.
Wealth and Poverty

BELL, ALEXANDER GRAHAM (1847–1922)

Scottish-American inventor best known for his invention of the telephone. Bell, who lived in Ontario, Canada, before coming to Boston, Massachusetts, started out as a teacher of the deaf. Because he could not make the parts he needed to create the telephone he envisioned, he had Thomas Watson, an electrician, help him create his now famous invention.
Cooperation and Unity

BENCHLEY, ROBERT (1889–1945)

U.S. humorist known for his essays and stories, many of which were published in *The New Yorker*.
Music

BENET, STEPHEN VINCENT (1898–1943)

U.S. author known for his poetry and short stories, many of which reflected his love of American history.
Compliments and Insults

BENNETT, GWENDOLYN (1902–1981)

U.S. artist and teacher. She wrote about art, African-American culture, and literature for a magazine called *Opportunity*.
Art

BERNHARDT, SARAH (1844–1923)

French actor who was one of the most famous stars of her time. She was such a convincing performer that she continued to play young, beautiful characters such as Juliet and Tosca when she was in her seventies.
Beauty

BERRA, YOGI (B. 1925)

U.S. baseball player and manager known for his funny observations, called Yogisms. His real name is Lawrence Peter Berra; he got his nickname from childhood friends, who insisted that he reminded them of a character named Yogi that they had seen in a movie.
Apologies and Excuses, Sports**, Travel and Adventure

BETHUNE, MARY MCLEOD (1875–1955)

U.S. educator who established Bethune-Cookman College in Florida, and served as advisor to several U.S. presidents. In 1936 she became the first African-American woman to head a federal agency.
Faith and Hope, History

BHUTTO, BENAZIR (B. 1953)

Pakistani prime minister who served from 1988–1990. She was the first woman ever elected as the leader of an Islamic nation.
History

BIBLE, THE

This book is considered the most sacred text in the Jewish and Christian religions. The Bible began as oral literature thousands of years ago, and different people from different cultures and faiths wrote down and preserved the text in different ways. The Hebrew Bible has 24 books or sections, the Protestant Bible has 66, and the Catholic Bible has 73. The biblical quotes in this book all come from the King James Bible, a form of the Protestant Bible that is most often used in literary quotations.

BIERCE, AMBROSE (1842–1914)
U.S. author known for his realistic war stories and eerie tales of horror as well as his humor.
Anger

BIG ELK (C. 1772–1846)
Omaha Chief known for his eloquence and his skill as a peacemaker. However, he did lead some war parties against the Pawnees.
Good Fortune and Misfortune

BIG THUNDER (BEDAGI) (LATE 19TH CENTURY)
Abenaki (Wapanaki) Algonquin leader whose words were recorded and later published in 1907 by Natalie Curtis in *The Indian's Book*.
Nature

BILLINGS, JOSH (1818–1885)
U.S. humorist who specialized in essays and short, clever sayings. His real name was Henry Wheeler Shaw but he used the name Josh Billings when he wrote and made speaking tours.
Action, Education and Learning, Food

BISMARCK, OTTO VON (1815–1898)
Prussian military leader who waged war to unite the German states into one empire.
Government and Politics

BLACK ELK (HEHAKA SAPA) (1863–1950)
Oglala Sioux spiritual leader whose life story was published as the book *Black Elk Speaks*.
Nature

BLAKE, WILLIAM (1757–1827)
British poet and artist who created pictures and poems full of symbolism and unusual images.
Change, Truth and Reality

BLUFORD, GUION (B. 1942)
U.S. astronaut who in 1983 became the first African-American to travel into space.
Travel and Adventure

BLUME, JUDY (B. 1938)
Popular U.S. author whose titles include *Tales of a Fourth Grade Nothing* and *Blubber*.
Advice

BOHR, NIELS (1885–1962)
Danish physicist who developed an important theory about the structure of the atom. He won the Nobel Prize in Physics in 1922.
Science and Technology

BOLÍVAR, SIMÓN (1783–1830)
South American revolutionary leader whose victories over the Spanish helped win independence for Bolivia, Columbia, Peru, Ecuador, and his homeland, Venezuela. He is remembered as the liberator of South America.
Freedom, Government and Politics

BONAPARTE, NAPOLEON SEE NAPOLEON I (1769–1821)

BORGE, VICTOR (B. 1909)
Danish-born U.S. comedian and pianist who combined classical piano concerts with comedy routines.
Humor

BORGES, JORGE LUIS (1899–1986)
Argentinean poet, critic, and fiction writer whose works are read all over the world.
Human Nature, Love and Hate, Writing

BOSWELL, JAMES (1740–1795)
Scottish author who is remembered for writing *The Life of Samuel Johnson.* He also kept detailed and witty personal journals in which he presented his opinions and experiences.
Compliments and Insults, Humor

BOURKE-WHITE, MARGARET (1906–1971)
U.S. photojournalist who often used a series of photos to present a subject. During World War II she photographed combat and the horrors of the Nazi concentration camps.
News and the Media

BOYNTON, SANDRA (B. 1953)
U.S. cartoonist whose humorous artwork appears in picture books and on greeting cards as well as in printed cartoons.
Food

BRADFORD, WILLIAM (1590–1657)
English-born governor of Plymouth Colony, Massachusetts. Under his leadership the colony survived many hardships, and he organized the celebration of the first Thanksgiving. His book *History of Plimmoth Plantation* provides a record of daily life in the colony.
Action, Time

BRADSTREET, ANNE (C. 1612–1672)
American Colonial poet whose book *The Tenth Muse Lately Sprung Up in America* was the first book of original poetry written in the American Colonies.
Good Fortune and Misfortune, Leaders and Leadership

BRILLAT-SAVARIN, ANTHELME (1755–1826)
French lawyer, author, and lover of fine foods. His book *The Physiology of Taste*, first published in 1825, is still read today for its detailed and amusing descriptions of his favorite meals and their preparation.
Food

BRONTË, CHARLOTTE (1816–1855)
British author of the famous *Jane Eyre* and of three other novels.
Action, Friendship and Loyalty, Home, Prejudice

BROOKE, RUPERT (1887–1915)
British poet who died while serving as a soldier during World War I. He is best known for a collection of poems called *1914*, containing patriotic sonnets about soldiers during wartime.
Citizenship and Patriotism

BROOKS, GWENDOLYN (B. 1917)
U.S. poet who in 1950 became the first African-American to win a Pulitzer Prize.
Language and Words, Writing

BROUN, HEYWOOD CAMPBELL
(1888–1939)
U.S. humorist known for his clever newspaper columns.
Food

BROWNING, ELIZABETH BARRETT
(1806–1861)
British poet who was among the most admired English poets of her time. Her most famous work, *Sonnets from the Portuguese,* was inspired by her love for her husband, Robert Browning. She also wrote works protesting child labor and political injustice.
*Love and Hate***

BROWNING, ROBERT (1812–1889)
British poet considered to be one of the greatest authors of his time. His poems often tell dramatic stories and present memorable characters.
Dreams and Goals, Effort and Enthusiasm, Old Age

BUDDHA (c. 563–483 B.C.)
Indian philosopher and founder of Buddhism. His name was Siddhartha Guatama. Buddha is a title of respect and means "the enlightened one." Buddha gave up a life of ease as a prince and devoted himself to teaching others how to overcome suffering.
Happiness and Sorrow, Right and Wrong

BULWER-LYTTON, EDWARD GEORGE
(1803–1873)
British novelist and playwright who often used characters and events from history in his work. He also served as a member of Parliament and was made a baron in 1866.
Language and Words

BUNCHE, RALPH (1904–1971)
U.S. diplomat who won the Nobel Prize for Peace in 1950 for his work in settling Arab-Israeli disputes in Palestine. He was the first African-American to win this award.
Peace

BURGESS, GELETT (1866–1951)
U.S. poet and humorist known for his playful rhymes and cartoons.
Art

BURKE, EDMUND (1729–1797)
British statesman who, during the American Revolution, urged the British government to grant the Colonists more rights to keep them part of the nation. He also worked to improve Irish-British relations.
Advice, Future, Government and Politics

BURNETT, FRANCES HODGSON
(1849–1924)
English-born U.S. author known for her books for children, including *The Secret Garden.*
Time

BURNS, ROBERT (1759–1796)
Scottish poet who was the national poet of Scotland and often used Scots dialect in his works.
Human Nature, Problems and Solutions, Self-Knowledge and Self-Respect

BUSH, BARBARA (B. 1925)

First lady of the U.S. who, as the wife of President George Bush, often spoke out on popular issues. She also wrote books and campaigned for literacy for all children.
Future

BYARS, BETSY (B. 1928)

U.S. author known for her popular children's books, including *The Summer of the Swans* and *The Midnight Fox*.
Writing

BYRON, LORD (1788–1824)

English poet known for his colorful and romantic poems and lifestyle. His full name and title was George Neal Gordon, 6th Baron Byron.
Beauty, Beginnings and Endings

CAESAR, JULIUS (100–44 B.C.)

Roman general whose military conquests helped build Rome into a powerful empire. The people of Rome appointed Caesar as their dictator for 10 years, but his political rivals feared Caesar wanted to be dictator of Rome for life and had him killed.
Choices, Confidence

CAGE, JOHN (1912–1992)

U.S. composer who experimented with many different and unusual sounds and techniques in the music he wrote.
Creativity and Ideas

CALDERÓN DE LA BARCA, PEDRO (1600–1681)

Spanish author known for his plays. He is considered the greatest Spanish playwright of his time.
Helping and Kindness

CALHOUN, JOHN C. (1782–1850)

U.S. politician from South Carolina who served as vice president from 1825 to 1832 and ran for president several times. He also served in the U.S. Congress, where, in an effort to protect the practice of slavery, he presented the theory of states' rights, rights that he claimed should allow states to reject national laws if they so chose.
Government and Politics

CALVIN, JOHN (1509–1564)

Swiss religious reformer who was one of the leaders of the Protestant Reformation. His views became important to the Church of England and in France and North America.
Time

CALVINO, ITALO (1923–1985)

Italian author who wrote science fiction, fantasy, and historical fiction. He also received great acclaim for his retelling of traditional tales in *Italian Folktales* (1956).
Books and Reading

CARLYLE, THOMAS (1795–1881)

Scottish author, philosopher, and historian whose most famous book presents his views on the French Revolution. Carlyle believed that heroes were special people who were stronger

and braver than others and were responsible for all advances in human progress.
Courage, Language and Words

CARNEGIE, ANDREW (1835–1919)
U.S. industrialist and philanthropist who made a fortune in the steel business. He also believed it was the duty of the rich to use some of their wealth to help others.
Dreams and Goals

CARNEGIE, DALE (1888–1955)
U.S. educator who offered courses on effective speaking and getting along with others. His book *How to Win Friends and Influence People* (1936) is still popular today.
Happiness and Sorrow

CARROLL, LEWIS (1832–1898)
British mathematician, clergyman, and author best known as the author of *Alice's Adventures in Wonderland* and *Through the Looking Glass*. His real name was Charles Lutwidge Dodgson.
Beginnings and Endings

CARSON, BENJAMIN (B. 1951)
U.S. surgeon and author who writes about his life experiences to inspire young African-Americans to aim high in life. As a surgeon, he is noted for his skill in treating children who require brain surgery.
Advice

CARSON, RACHEL (1907–1964)
U.S. scientist and author of *The Silent Spring* and other books about nature and the environment.
Nature**

CARTER, JIMMY (B. 1924)
Thirty-ninth president of the United States and former governor of Georgia. During and after his presidency he often assisted the U.S. and other nations in solving problems related to human rights. His full name is James Earl Carter, Jr.
Justice and Equality, Nature

CARUSO, ENRICO (1873–1921)
Italian opera singer who was known for his ability to hold notes for a long time and the emotion he put into his tenor voice. When he was not singing, he was known for his knack to speak plainly and enjoy simple things.
Food

CARVER, GEORGE WASHINGTON (C. 1864–1943)
U.S. botanist whose agricultural research changed the way people grew crops (especially sweet potatoes and peanuts) all over the world. He was born a slave and worked his way through school. In 1896 he went to teach at the Tuskegee Institute in Alabama and in 1910 he became head of its Department of Research.
Apologies and Excuses, Curiosity, Science and Technology

CASALS, PABLO (1876–1973)
Spanish cellist who also worked as a composer and conductor and is considered one the greatest musicians of his time. Although he was born and raised in Spain, he moved to Puerto Rico in 1956. There he continued his

active career in music until the end of his long life.
Old Age

CATHER, WILLA (1873–1947)
U.S. author whose fiction brings to life the landscape and people of Nebraska and the Southwest. Her most famous books include *O Pioneers!* and *My Ántonia.*
Experience, Travel and Adventures

CATHERINE II (1729–1796)
Empress of Russia known also as Catherine the Great. She was a German princess who at sixteen married Peter, a Russian prince. In 1762 she and others decided that her husband, who was now the czar of Russia, was not fit to rule. Catherine took the throne as empress of the land. Under her leadership, Russia became a world power. She built schools and hospitals and promoted the arts, education for women, and religious tolerance; but she did little to give greater freedom to the Russian people.
Leaders and Leadership

CATHERINE OF SIENA, SAINT (1347–1380)
Italian religious reformer who was known for her charity, diplomatic skills, and ability to influence Pope Gregory XI. Due to her persuasion, the pope moved the capitol of the Roman Catholic Church from Avignon, France, back to Rome.
Good Fortune and Misfortune

CATO THE ELDER (234–149 B.C.)
Roman statesman known for his conservative views and his opposition to any kind of

change. He wanted to bring simplicity to Roman life.
Anger

CATT, CARRIE CHAPMAN (1859–1947)
U.S. advocate for women's rights whose work extended from the United States to Canada and Europe. In 1920 she founded the National League of Women Voters.
Government

CERVANTES, MIGUEL DE (1547–1616)
Spanish author of *Don Quixote,* the classic novel about a man who imagines he is a knight in armor and goes off to fight injustice.
Food, Truth and Reality

CHAMFORT, SÉBASTIEN ROCH NICOLAS (1741–1794)
French author known for his witty and humorous descriptions of people and events.
Humor

CHANDRASEKHAR, SUBRAHMANYAN (1910–1995)
Indian-born U.S. Nobel-prizewinning astrophysicist best known for his study of white dwarf stars—stars that are billions and billions of years old.
Truth and Reality

CHANNING, WILLIAM ELLERY (1780–1842)
U.S. Unitarian minister who worked for world peace and the abolition of slavery.
Education and Learning

CHARLEMAGNE (742–814)

King of the Franks, an ancient Germanic people who began attacking the Roman Empire around A.D. 200. Charlemagne, who was also known as Charles the Great, conquered and united most of Western Europe. By 800, his empire extended from Italy to Denmark and Pope Leo III crowned him emperor of the Romans. After Charlemagne's death, the Frankish empire began to break up into what later became the kingdoms of Germany, Italy, and France.
Food

CHARLES I (1600–1649)

King of England whose rule was marked by political and religious conflict and civil war. He was convicted of treason by Parliament and beheaded.
Apologies and Excuses

CHAUCER, GEOFFREY (C. 1343–1400)

British writer who is considered the greatest English poet of his time. His famous work *The Canterbury Tales* is a collection of stories told in rhyme about a group of pilgrims on a journey.
Beauty, Friendship and Loyalty, Time

CHAVEZ, CESAR (1927–1993)

U.S. labor leader for migrant farmers who began to organize California grape pickers in 1962 to ask for better working conditions. He urged boycotts of grapes and lettuce to show popular support for farm workers when they were negotiating for better contracts.
Justice and Equality

CHEN, WU SEE WU CHEN

CHESTERFIELD, LORD (1694–1773)

British diplomat and author known for his letters, which were published after his death. When his son was five years old, Chesterfield began writing him letters filled with advice. He continued for 30 years, hoping his letters would educate his son on the art of being a gentleman. His full name and title was Philip Dormer Stanhope, Earl of Chesterfield.
Community and City Life, Human Nature, Time

CHIANG KAI-SHEK, MADAME SEE SOONG MEI LING

CHIEF JOSEPH SEE JOSEPH, CHIEF

CHIEF SEATTLE SEE SEATTLE, CHIEF

CHILDRESS, ALICE (1920–1994)

African-American actress, playwright, and novelist who won critical acclaim for her work. Her young adult novel *A Hero Ain't Nothin' but a Sandwich* is among her most popular works.
Human Nature

CHINGHIZ KHAN SEE GENGHIS KHAN

CHISHOLM, SHIRLEY (B. 1924)

U.S. Congressperson and former teacher who in 1969 became the first African-American to be elected to Congress. She published her autobiography, *Unbought and Unbossed* in 1970.
Leaders and Leadership

CHRISTIE, AGATHA (1890–1976)

British author known for her detective novels featuring detectives Miss Marple and Hercule

Poirot. She was made Dame Commander in the Order of the British Empire in 1971.
Problems and Solutions

CHUANG-TZU (C. 369–C. 287 B.C.)
Chinese philosopher who was also a master of Taoism. He often used humor to get his ideas across. His name is sometimes spelled Zhaungzi.
Happiness and Sorrow

CHURCHILL, WINSTON (1874–1965)
British prime minister and statesman who led his people through World War II. He started his career as a soldier and reporter and was first elected to Parliament in 1900. In addition to his active life in politics, Churchill also wrote books, winning the Nobel Prize in Literature in 1953. He also found time to pursue the hobby of painting.
Animals, Art, Compliments and Insults, Effort and Enthusiasm, Government and Politics, War

CICERO, MARCUS TULLIUS (106–43 B.C.)
Roman orator, poet, and statesman who wrote and spoke on many topics. His opinions sometimes got him into trouble and finally led to his death. He was killed by the Second Triumvirate (the three coleaders of Rome) because he opposed their rule.
Advice, Faith and Hope, History, Justice and Equality

CLARKE, ARTHUR C. (B. 1917)
British science-fiction writer whose books often predicted actual scientific advancements,

such as communication satellites. His novel *2001: a Space Odyssey* was made into a movie.
Creativity and Ideas

CLAY, CASSIUS SEE ALI, MUHAMMED

CLAY, HENRY (1777–1852)
U.S. Senator from Kentucky known as the Great Compromiser because he often helped to settle conflicts about slavery between Northern and Southern states.
Choices, Government and Politics

CLEMENCEAU, GEORGES (1841–1929)
French politician who led France as its premier during the last, difficult years of World War I.
War

CLEMENS, SAMUEL LANGHORNE SEE TWAIN, MARK

CLIFTON, LUCILLE (B. 1936)
U.S. poet and author of more than 20 books for adults and children that reflect the African-American experience.
Wealth and Poverty

CLINTON, HILLARY RODHAM (B. 1947)
First lady of the U.S. who wrote the best-selling book *It Takes a Village*. The title of her book comes from a proverb from Benin, West Africa, and every chapter in her book begins with a proverb or quotation. She had an active career as a lawyer before she became first lady.
Community and City Life

CLINTON, WILLIAM (B. 1946)
42nd president of the United States and former governor of Arkansas. Clinton, a

Democrat, was elected president first in 1992, defeating George Bush, and again in 1996 when he ran against Robert Dole.
Citizenship and Patriotism

COKE, SIR EDWARD (1552–1634)
British chief justice of the Court of Common Pleas who was the most influential judge of his day.
Home

COLLINS, MARVA (B. 1936)
U.S. educator who often speaks out on issues regarding urban education and African-American youth.
Education and Learning

COLTON, CHARLES CALEB (1780–1832)
British poet and essayist, among his best remembered works is *Lacon* (1820).
Advice, Compliments and Insults, Prejudice

CONAN DOYLE, ARTHUR SEE DOYLE, SIR ARTHUR CONAN

CONFUCIUS (551–479 B.C.)
Chinese philosopher whose ideas had great influence on the development of culture and ethics in China, Japan, Korea, and Vietnam. Although no books written by Confucius have been found, his sayings and teachings were recorded by his students in *The Analects*.
Advice, Change, Leaders and Leadership, Right and Wrong

CONGREVE, WILLIAM (1670–1729)
British playwright who wrote many comedies. However, his famous quote about music comes from the one tragedy he wrote, *The Mourning Bride*.
Music

COOK, JAMES (1728–1779)
British navigator who made voyages to the Pacific, leading expeditions to Tahiti, Australia, Antarctica, and New Zealand.
Travel and Adventure

COOLIDGE, CALVIN (1872–1933)
Thirtieth president of the United States, who led the United States during the 1920s. He was known for his common sense and for making his statements brief.
Citizenship and Patriotism

COSBY, BILL (B. 1937)
U.S. actor and author known for his comedy, which often focuses on family life.
Success

COWPER, WILLIAM (1731–1800)
British poet who often wrote about nature and the charms of daily life. He also wrote many hymns, including "Light Shining out of Darkness," from which his famous quote comes.
Faith and Hope

CROCKETT, DAVID (1786–1836)
U.S. frontiersman, politician, and soldier who often used exaggeration when he talked about his abilities and adventures. Crockett served in the Tennessee legislature and then represented Tennessee in the United States Senate. He died in the battle of the Alamo in Texas when

Mexican forces overpowered those fighting for independence from Mexico.
Advice, Confidence

CURIE, MARIE (1867–1934)
Polish-born French scientist who won two Nobel Prizes for her research on radioactive materials. Along with her husband, Pierre, she discovered two new elements, radium and polonium.
Achievements, Curiosity, Science and Technology

DA VINCI, LEONARDO SEE LEONARDO DA VINCI

DAHL, ROALD (1916–1990)
British author known for eerie adult stories and his funny and fantastic novels for children, including *James and the Giant Peach, Charlie and the Chocolate Factory,* and *Matilda.*
Family, Writing

DALI, SALVADOR (1904–1989)
Spanish painter known for his paintings, which show strange combinations of objects and people.
Art

DANA, CHARLES A. (1819–1897)
U.S. journalist who was the part owner and the editor of the *New York Sun,* one of the most influential newspapers of the late 1800s.
News and the Media

DANG DUNG (C. 1750)
Vietnamese patriot who fought against Chinese rule of his homeland. "Regrets," the

only poem he wrote that survived him, is still read today.
Good Fortune and Misfortune

DANTE (1265–1321)
Italian author best remembered for *The Divine Comedy,* a book-length poem that tells of an imaginary journey the author takes through Hell, Purgatory, and Paradise. His full name was Dante Alighieri.
Nature

DANZIGER, PAULA (B. 1944)
U.S. author of many popular novels for young adults, including *The Pistachio Prescription* and *This Place Has No Atmosphere.* She is also the author of the popular series about a girl named Amber Brown.
Food

DARROW, CLARENCE (1857–1938)
U.S. lawyer known for his clever defense in criminal trials. He also defended labor unions, and in 1925 he defended the right of John Scopes to teach the theory of evolution in a Tennessee public school.
Character, Freedom

DARWIN, CHARLES (1809–1882)
British scientist who became famous for his theories on evolution by natural selection. He studied variations among plants and animals and used what he observed to support his theories.
Music, Science and Technology

DAVIES, ROBERTSON (1913–1995)
Canadian author of novels, plays, and newspaper columns. He is considered Canada's

leading English language author of his era. He was born William Robertson Davies.
Books and Reading, Truth and Reality

DAVIS, OSSIE (B. 1917)
U.S. actor who has starred on stage and screen in drama and comedies about African-American life. He is also the author of plays and novels for young adults.
Advice

DEAN, DIZZY (1911–1974)
U.S. baseball player known for his colorful personality and his skill as a pitcher. He quit school after the second grade and picked cotton and worked at other jobs before becoming a professional baseball player in 1930. He played for the St. Louis Cardinals and then the Chicago Cubs. Later he worked as a sports announcer on radio and TV.
Confidence

DECATUR, STEPHEN (1779–1820)
U.S. naval officer who led daring campaigns against the enemies of the United States in various wars from 1798–1820.
Citizenship and Patriotism

DEGAS, EDGAR (1834–1917)
French painter and sculptor known for portraits, which capture the humanity of his subjects. He studied Renaissance paintings and Japanese prints as he developed his own style.
Art

DELANY, BESSIE (1891–1995)
U.S. dentist and author who, with her sister Sadie (see below), published her memoirs and observations about life in a book called *Having Our Say.* Both sisters were past the age of one hundred when they wrote the book.
Change

DELANY, SADIE (B. 1889)
U.S. educator and co-author of *Having Our Say.* The Delany sisters were the daughters of the first black Episcopal minister in New York and knew many of the prominent authors and artists of the Harlem Renaissance. At the age of one hundred seven, Sadie published a new book called *On My Own,* about how she coped with the death of her sister Bessie.
Advice, Time

DELILLE, JACQUES (1738–1813)
French poet who was considered the greatest poet of his time. In addition to writing original poems, he translated great works by other poets into French, including Virgil's *Aeneid* and Milton's *Paradise Lost.*
Friendship and Loyalty

DESCARTES, RENÉ (1596–1650)
French philosopher and mathematician who believed the world was made up of Matter (the physical world) and Spirit (the human mind).
Ability and Talent, Creativity and Ideas

DHAMMAPADA (C. 3RD CENTURY)
This Buddhist text from India contains over 400 wise sayings to help readers lead a moral life and follow the appropriate path to enlightenment.
Introduction, Love and Hate

DICKENS, CHARLES (1812–1870)

British novelist whose works, including *A Tale of Two Cities, A Christmas Carol,* and *Oliver Twist,* are still popular today.
*Helping and Kindness, History**, Wealth and Poverty*

DICKINSON, EMILY (1830–1886)

U.S. poet who wrote over 1,700 poems but published very few during her lifetime. She was a very private person and in the latter half of her life seldom went out or saw anyone other than her family. Her poems are usually short and present her unique observations on nature and life and death.
Animals, Creativity and Ideas, Faith and Hope, Home, Language and Words, Success, Truth and Reality

DIOGENES (C. 400–C. 325 B.C.)

Greek philosopher who was part of a school of philosophers called Cynics. They believed that people should devote their lives to practicing self-control and freeing themselves from personal pleasures.
Language and Words

DISNEY, WALT (1901–1966)

U.S. cartoonist and filmmaker who created Mickey Mouse and Donald Duck, among other popular characters. His full-length cartoon features include *Snow White and the Seven Dwarfs* and *Pinocchio.* He did much of the writing for his early films.
Dreams and Goals

DISRAELI, BENJAMIN (1804–1881)

British statesman and prime minister who was the first British prime minister of Jewish ancestry. He played an important role in the passage of the Reform Bill of 1867, which gave the vote to many working-class British people. He also wrote several novels in which politics were important to the plots.
Books and Reading, Greatness, Justice and Equality

DONNE, JOHN (1572–1631)

British poet and Anglican priest. He became famous for his sermons and preached often in the royal court. His poem "Death Be Not Proud" is part of a series of Holy Sonnets he wrote toward the end of his life.
Animals, Community and City Life

DOUGLASS, FREDERICK (1817–1895)

U.S. and Canadian journalist and civil rights leader who used his writing and his eloquence as a public speaker to campaign for the rights of African-Americans. He was born Frederick Bailey and spent his earliest years as a slave in Maryland. He changed his name when he ran away in 1838 and secured his own freedom.
Education and Learning, Effort and Enthusiasm, Freedom, Truth and Reality

DOYLE, SIR ARTHUR CONAN (1859–1930)

British writer remembered as the creator of the great fiction detective, Sherlock Holmes. In his many adventures, Holmes uses logic and his extraordinary powers of observation to solve baffling mysteries.
Truth and Reality

DR. SEUSS SEE SEUSS, DR.

DU BOIS, W.E.B. (1868–1963)
U.S. and Ghanaian civil rights leader, educator, and journalist who won fame for his research and published writings in history and sociology. He believed that all people of African descent had common interests and some shared heritage and needed to work together against racism. In 1895 he became the first black scholar to receive a Ph.D. from Harvard University. Discouraged with what he considered the slow advancement of civil rights in the U.S., he moved to Ghana in 1961. His full name was William Edward Burghardt Du Bois.
Citizenship and Patriotism, Dreams and Goals

DUMAS, ALEXANDRE (1802–1870)
French author of European and African descent whose famous romantic novels include *The Three Musketeers* and *The Count of Monte Cristo*. He also wrote plays that were popular in his day.
Cooperation and Unity, Loneliness and Solitude, Success, Wisdom

DURANT, WILL (1885–1981) AND ARIEL DURANT (1898–1981)
U.S. historians who were married and worked as a team to write an 11-volume work called *The Story of Civilization*.
History

EARHART, AMELIA (1898–1937)
U.S. aviator who was the first female pilot to fly across the Atlantic. She disappeared mysteriously over the Pacific Ocean as she attempted to set a new record for an around-the-world flight.
Beginnings and Endings

EBAN, ABBA (B. 1915)
Israeli statesman who served as his nation's first ambassador to the United Nations. He also held several other important posts in the Israeli government, including deputy prime minister.
History

EDELMAN, MARIAN WRIGHT (B. 1939)
U.S. lawyer and children's rights activist who in 1973 founded the Children's Defense Fund, which works on getting funding for programs for children and families. Earlier in her career she headed the NAACP Legal Defense and Educational Fund.
Community and City Life, Youth

EDGEWORTH, MARIA (1767–1849)
Irish essayist and novelist of *Tales of a Fashionable Life* and other books.
Helping and Kindness

EDISON, THOMAS ALVA (1847–1931)
U.S. inventor who patented 1,093 inventions during his lifetime, including the electric light, the phonograph, and one of the first successful motion-picture machines. Edison became deaf as an adult, possibly because of a childhood injury. Although an operation could have improved his hearing, Edison declined to have surgery, saying his deafness made it easier for him to concentrate.
Effort and Enthusiasm, Science and Technology

EDWARD III (1312–1377)

King of England who invaded Scotland and began the first battles of what was to become the Hundred Years War with France.
Government and Politics

EDWARDS, JONATHAN (1703–1758)

Calvinist preacher in Puritan New England. His sermons often left his audiences shaking with fear. He stressed what would happen to "sinners in the hands of an angry God." He also published his Resolutions, rules for how he and others could lead a good and moral life.
Dreams and Goals

EINSTEIN, ALBERT (1879–1955)

German-born U.S. scientist considered to be one of the most creative scientists of any age. He is best known for his theory of relativity, which revolutionized the way scientists thought about energy, matter, time, and space. His theories advanced studies of atomic energy and space travel.
Creativity and Ideas, Future, Mathematics, Science and Technology, Success, Truth and Reality

EISENHOWER, DWIGHT D. (1890–1969)

Thirty-fourth president of United States who, before becoming president, led the U.S. forces in Europe during World War II. When he was president, he was often photographed playing golf; however, he also loved football. As a young cadet at the U.S. Military Academy at West Point, he played for the school's football team until a knee injury forced him to retire from the sport.
Sports

ELIOT, GEORGE (1819–1880)

British author of *Silas Marner* and other novels about English country life. Her real name was Mary Ann or Marian Evans, but she used the name George Eliot when she wrote because the people of her day expected the authors of novels to be men, not women.
Animals

ELIOT, T. S. (1888–1965)

U.S.-born British poet whose collection of playful poems *Old Possum's Book of Practical Cats* became the foundation for the musical production *Cats*. Most of his other poetry was far from lighthearted and used complex structures and themes. He won the Nobel Prize in Literature in 1948. His full name was Thomas Stearns Eliot.
Animals, Home, News and the Media

ELIZABETH I (1533–1603)

Queen of England who ruled from 1558 until her death. During her reign, England became a major economic and naval power. English literature also flourished during her rule.
Language and Words, Old Age

EMERSON, RALPH WALDO (1803–1882)

U.S. essayist, minister, and philosopher who believed in being true to oneself as an individual and that others are also capable of doing good. His beliefs about nature and life were shared by others, who called themselves transcendentalists. His ideas influenced other great writers, including Louisa May Alcott,

Henry David Thoreau, Walt Whitman, and Emily Dickinson.

Achievements, Art, Change, Community and City Life, Dreams and Goals, Education and Learning, Effort and Enthusiasm, Friendship and Loyalty**, Good Fortune and Misfortune, Greatness, Manners, Nature, Science and Technology, Self-Knowledge and Self-Respect, Work

ENNIUS (239–169 B.C.)

Roman historian and poet. His most important work was the *Annales*, a history of Rome from the time of the Trojan War until his own time. His full name was Quintus Ennius.

Friendship and Loyalty, Good Fortune and Misfortune

ERDRICH, LOUISE (B. 1954)

U.S. author of Chippewa (Ojibwa) descent whose novels, poetry, and essays often explore the lives of people of Native American heritage and of strong women.

Love and Hate, Wealth and Poverty

EURIPIDES (C. 485–406 B.C.)

Greek playwright known for his tragedies, plays in which the hero meets a terrible end due to some flaw in his character.

Ability and Talent, Effort and Enthusiasm

EVANS, MARY ANN SEE ELIOT, GEORGE

EVERS, MEDGAR (1926–1963)

U.S. civil rights leader who served as field secretary for the NAACP (National Association for the Advancement of Colored People) and worked to end segregation at the University of Mississippi and to encourage African-Americans to vote. Evers was killed by a sniper's bullet in front of his own home.

Creativity and Ideas

FADIMAN, CLIFTON (B. 1904)

U.S. author, journalist, and humorist whose books include *Any Number Can Play*.

Books and Reading, Food

FARRAGUT, DAVID GLASGOW (1801–1870)

U.S. naval officer who became famous during the Civil War with the slogan "Damn the torpedoes! Full speed ahead." While at sea, he wrote many letters to his wife that revealed his thoughts about all aspects of life.

Success

FENWICK, MILLICENT (1910–1992)

U.S. politician who represented New Jersey in the House of Representatives from 1975–1982.

Manners

FISHER, DOROTHY CANFIELD (1879–1958)

U.S. author of essays and fiction, including *Her Son's Wife*.

Family

FITZGERALD, ELLA (1917–1996)

U.S. jazz singer called "The First Lady of Song." She was known for her original interpretations of many popular songs. At seventeen, she won an Amateur Night Contest at the legendary Apollo Theater, where many great African-American musicians started on the road to success. Her long career included

many solo performances and recordings as well as concerts with other leading musicians.
Music

FLAUBERT, GUSTAVE (1821–1880)
French novelist whose best-known work was also his first book, *Madame Bovary.* This book caused a scandal when it was first published in 1857, but it also brought Flaubert fame. He developed a new and distinctive style of writing, inspiring many French authors to change the way they wrote by adding more realistic details.
Writing

FOLEY, J. (1905–1970)
British songwriter who published his version of a popular British army song in 1920.
Old Age

FORD, HENRY (1863–1947)
U.S. automobile manufacturer who revolutionized automobile production and amassed a great fortune by using assembly-line methods.
Creativity and Ideas, Problems and Solutions

FRANK, ANNE (1929–1945)
German-Jewish girl whose diary revealed her thoughts and feelings as she lived in hiding from the Nazis during World War II. Although she was eventually captured and died in a concentration camp, her diary was published after her death and is still read today.
Character, Human Nature

FRANKLIN, BENJAMIN (1706–1790)
American statesman, inventor, and writer who is remembered for the role he played in the building of the new government of the United States; his inventions, including bifocal eyeglasses and the Franklin stove; and his clever observations, recorded in his autobiography and in *Poor Richard's Almanac.*
Advice**, Anger, Apologies and Excuses, Compliments and Insults, Cooperation and Unity, Faith and Hope, Freedom, Happiness and Sorrow, Success, Time, War, Wealth and Poverty

FROST, ROBERT (1874–1963)
U.S. poet who was the most popular poet of his time. In 1960 Congress gave Frost a gold medal "in recognition of his poetry, which has enriched the culture of the United States and the philosophy of the world." Many of his poems include details that relate to the New England landscape and people he loved.
Choices, Community and City Life, Responsibility

FULLER, BUCKMINSTER (1895–1983)
U.S. engineer and inventor who is best known for designing large geodesic domes, structures that look like giant golf balls when seen from afar. He believed that a good designer worked in cooperation with nature and that technology and careful planning could be used to solve any problem.
Nature

FULLER, THOMAS (1608–1661)
British clergyman and author of histories and religious texts whose works include *A Pisgah-Sight of Palestine* and *Life of the Duke of Alva.*
Compliments and Insults, Faith and Hope

FULLER, THOMAS (1654–1734)

British physician and author whose works include *Gnomologia,* a collection of knowledge.
Education and Learning

GALSWORTHY, JOHN (1867–1933)

British novelist and playwright who won the Nobel Prize in Literature in 1932. His best known work is *The Forsyte Saga*, a series of three novels about a character named Soames Fosyte. His plays include *Justice* and *Loyalties*.
Justice and Equality

GANDHI, INDIRA (1917–1984)

First woman prime minister of India, who held that office from 1966 to 1977 and from 1980 until the end of her life. She was the only child of Jawaharlal Nehru, India's first prime minister.
Leaders and Leadership, Peace, Work

GANDHI, MOHANDAS (1869–1948)

Indian leader called Mahatma (meaning great soul) by his followers. He worked for decades to free India from British rule. Gandhi believed in achieving goals through nonviolent actions. His life and writings inspired other great civil rights leaders, including Martin Luther King, Jr.
Courage, Peace

GARIBALDI, GIUSEPPE (1807–1882)

Italian nationalist and military hero who fought to create a united, independent Italian state. Earlier conquests by the French and Germans as well as small kingdoms within Italy had kept the Italian people divided for many years under the rule of leaders who did not have their best interests at heart. Garibaldi and his small army of patriotic volunteers, called Red Shirts, captured Sicily and Naples to help create the Kingdom of Italy in 1861.
Citizenship and Patriotism

GARVEY, MARCUS (1887–1940)

Jamaican civil rights leader who believed that all people of African descent should consider Africa their homeland. He started a "Back to Africa" movement in the U.S. in the early 1920s and had about two million followers.
Confidence

GATES, WILLIAM III (B. 1955)

U.S. computer and software expert who is among the wealthiest people in the world. He developed many new innovations in computer software and systems and founded and manages the company Microsoft.
Science and Technology

GENGHIS KHAN (C. 1162–1227)

Mongol warrior and conqueror who united the Mongols and invaded and conquered northern China and lands that are now Iran, Iraq, and part of Russia. His name is sometimes spelled Chingiz Khan.
Beginnings and Endings

GEORGE, JEAN CRAIGHEAD (B. 1919)

U.S. author known for her books for young people, which are filled with information about animals and life in the wild. Her award-winning titles include *Julie of the Wolves* and *My Side of the Mountain.*
Animals

GERSHWIN, GEORGE (1898–1937)
U.S. composer whose most famous works include *Porgy and Bess, Rhapsody in Blue*, and *An American in Paris*. He also wrote the music for a number of Broadway musicals.
Music

GIBRAN, KAHLIL (1883–1931)
Syrian-born U.S. author who wrote in both Arabic and English. His book *The Prophet* (1923) reached a wide audience. He also was an accomplished painter known for his portraits.
Helping and Kindness, Truth and Reality

GIBSON, ALTHEA (B. 1927)
U.S. tennis star who was the first African-American to win all the world's women's singles titles. Early in her career she received much need financial support and encouragement from leading African-American business people and sports stars. She retired from tennis in 1958 and then became a professional golfer.
Helping and Kindness

GILBERT, SIR W. S. (1836–1911)
British lyricist who with his partner, composer Arthur Sullivan, wrote many popular light operas for the British stage, including *H.M.S. Pinafore* and *The Mikado*. His full name was Sir William Schwenck Gilbert.
Food, Truth and Reality

GIOVANNI, NIKKI (B. 1943)
U.S. poet, essayist, and author of children's books. Her full name is Yolande Cornelia Giovanni, Jr. Much of her work focuses on the experiences of African-American women.
Experience, Self-Knowledge and Self-Respect, Truth and Reality

GOETHE, JOHANN WOLFGANG VON (1749–1832)
German poet, playwright, and philosopher whose most famous work is his play *Faust,* the story of a man who wants to know and experience everything about life.
Action, Home, Creativity and Ideas

GOLDWYN, SAMUEL (1882–1974)
U.S. film producer who helped create some of the most successful Hollywood films from the 1930s through the 1950s. Goldwin was born in Poland and at the age of thirteen he emigrated alone to the U.S.
Effort and Enthusiasm

GONZALES, RODOLFO "CORKY" (B. 1928)
U.S. civil rights leader and poet who encourages Mexican-Americans to take pride in their heritage. In 1965 he founded the Crusade for Justice, a Denver social action group that provides legal and medical aid. In 1967 he printed and handed out his epic poem "I Am Joaquin." This poem, which celebrates the history, strength, and endurance of Chicanos in the face of many hardships, became so popular that it was published in book form in 1972.
Self-Knowledge and Self-Respect

GOOSE, MOTHER
The rhymes that are associated with Mother Goose today were not written by any one

person. *Mother Goose's Melody* was a collection of traditional and popular English rhymes first published by John Newbery in 1781. Since then there have been many different collections of Mother Goose rhymes. However, some historians believe that Mother Goose was a real person, perhaps the mother of Charlemagne, whose nickname was "Queen Goose-foot." In France, as early as 1650, classic folktales such as "Cinderella" were called Mother Goose tales. Newbery chose the name Mother Goose for his collection of rhymes because he had previously translated and published the French *Mother Goose Tales* with great success.
Action

GORBACHEV, MIKHAIL (B. 1931)
President of the former USSR, who won the Nobel Prize for Peace in 1990 in recognition of the work he did to bring about reforms within his country and to improve international relations.
History

GORDIMER, NADINE (B. 1923)
South African author who won acclaim for her novels, which portrayed the negative effects of living under apartheid. This system had black and white South Africans living separately and afforded far fewer opportunities to black South Africans.
Truth and Reality

GRAHAM, MARTHA (1894–1991)
U.S. dancer and choreographer credited with creating a movement called modern dance. She used the entire body as the dancer's instrument to express all the feelings of the character he or she was portraying.
Dance

GRAHAM, PHILIP (1915–1963)
U.S. newspaper publisher who ran *The Washington Post.*
News and the Media

GRANT, ULYSSES S. (1822–1885)
Eighteenth president of the United States, who also led the Union troops to victory in the Civil War. He worked hard at many different jobs, from farming to rent collecting, with little success until he volunteered for military service in 1861. Although he had no political experience, he was elected president in 1868 because he was a popular hero.
Work

GRETSKY, WAYNE (B. 1961)
Canadian hockey player who is considered a great scorer. He has played for leading National Hockey League teams in Canada and the United States.
Sports

GRIMKÉ, CHARLOTTE FORTEN
(1837–1914)
U.S. educator who was the granddaughter of James Forten, a free black and a leading businessman and advocate for the rights of African-Americans in Colonial days. Charlotte became the first black teacher in the Sea Islands of South Carolina to help educate former slaves after the Civil War.
Language and Words

GUEST, EDGAR (1881–1959)
U.S. poet and journalist who was born in England and came to the U.S. as a child. His poetry, which often included lines written in folksy dialect, celebrated the everyday joys of friendship, family, and home.
Advice, Home

GUEVARA, CHE (1928–1967)
Argentinean-born revolutionary leader whose given name was Ernesto but preferred the nickname Che. Although he had trained to become a doctor, he believed that overthrowing ineffective governments was the only way to improve the lives of the people. He took an active role in helping Fidel Castro take over Cuba and spent several years as a powerful governmental official in Cuba after Castro seized control.
Action

GUPPY, SHUSHA (B. 1938)
Persian writer, singer, and songwriter who was born in Iran. In 1988 she published *The Blindfold Horse: Memoirs of a Persian Childhood*.
Music

GUTHRIE, WOODY (1912–1967)
U.S. folksinger and composer who wrote more than 1,000 songs, including the classic "This Land is Your Land." His full name was Woodrow Wilson Guthrie.
Music

HALE, EDWARD EVERETT (1822–1909)
U.S. clergyman, author, and humanitarian who founded the first Lend a Hand Club in Boston, which focused on charitable works. He was the grandnephew of Nathan Hale.
Action

HALE, NATHAN (1755–1776)
American Revolutionary soldier who volunteered to serve as a spy behind British lines. He was captured and sentenced to hang. According to tradition, he made a speech before his execution. The famous quotation from that speech is included in this book.
Citizenship and Patriotism

HALE, SARAH JOSEPHA (1788–1879)
U.S. author and editor of leading women's magazines. She is credited with persuading President Lincoln to establish Thanksgiving as a national holiday. She is also remembered as the author of "Mary Had a Little Lamb."
Citizenship and Patriotism

HALEY, ALEX (1921–1992)
U.S. author of *Roots* (1976), the powerful saga in which he described his own family's history, beginning in Gambia and then moving to the U.S. when his ancestor Kunta Kinte was sold into slavery.
Family, Helping and Kindness

HAMILTON, ALEXANDER (1755–1804))
American Colonial statesman who served as part of President George Washington's Cabinet as the first Secretary of the Treasury of the U.S. Earlier, with John Jay and James Madison, he wrote *The Federalist Papers,* letters which stressed the importance of adopting the new Constitution.
Time

HAMILTON, VIRGINIA (B. 1936)
U.S. author of works for children and young adults acclaimed for her powerful novels and folklore about African-American life and world culture, including *The People Could Fly* and *M.C. Higgins the Great*.
Community and City Life, Writing

HAMMERSTEIN, OSCAR II (1895–1960)
U.S. songwriter who wrote the lyrics and scripts for many classic musical theater shows, including *Oklahoma!* and *Showboat*. Among his most famous songs is "Oh, What a Beautiful Mornin'," which celebrates nature on a morning in Oklahoma.
Nature

HAMMURABI (D. 1750 B.C.)
Babylonian king who ruled from 1792 B.C. until his death. He developed one of the first comprehensive codes of laws used by a government. The Code of Hammurabi was based on older collections of laws which this great king revised and expanded. It contains over 300 provisions that stress fairness and that the strong shall not injure the weak.
Justice and Equality

HAND, LEARNED (1872–1961)
U.S. judge who served from 1924–1951 on the U.S. Court of Appeals. He became famous for his careful reasoning and well-explained legal rulings.
News and the Media

HANDY, W. C. (1873–1958)
U. S. blues musician who performed with bands and wrote and published his own songs, including "The Saint Louis Blues." Born William Christopher Handy, he began playing the trumpet and the piano when he was quite young. This African-American musician is remembered as the "father of the blues."
Effort and Enthusiasm

HANNIBAL (247–183 B.C.)
Military leader and statesman of Carthage who almost defeated powerful Rome in the Second Punic War. Known for his bold, creative military plans, he took his troops, horses, and some elephants on a bold maneuver across the Pyrenees and Alps to attack the Romans in the Po valley of what is now Italy.
Problems and Solutions

HANSBERRY, LORRAINE (1930–1965)
U.S. playwright and essayist whose promising career was cut short when she died of cancer at the age of thirty-four. Her most famous works include the play *A Raisin in the Sun* and the collection of her writings entitled *To Be Young Gifted and Black*.
Introduction, Creativity and Ideas

HATSHEPSUT (1503–1482 B.C.)
Pharaoh of ancient Egypt who ruled as co-regent with her husband and half-brother, Thutmose II, and later, after his death, assumed the full powers of pharaoh. She is remembered for commissioning the building of a great temple, in Deir el-Bahri, near Thebes.
Leaders and Leadership

HATUN, MIHRI (D. 1506)
Turkish poet who had great influence on the intellectual circles of the first Ottoman Empire.
Love and Hate

HAVEL, VÁCLAV (B. 1936)
Czech leader who became president of his country in 1989 and was the first noncommunist leader the nation had since 1948. He is also a playwright whose plays explore issues of human rights.
Citizenship and Patriotism

HAWTHORNE, NATHANIEL (1804–1864)
U.S. author of many short stories and novels, including *The Scarlet Letter*. He wanted his writing to show the reality of how people think and behave, saying he wanted to express "the depths of our common nature."
Human Nature

HAY, JOHN (1838–1905)
U.S. diplomat, statesman, and author, who wrote editorials for *The New York Tribune* before becoming involved with foreign policy as an ambassador and later secretary of state of the U.S.
Good Fortune and Misfortune

HAYAKAWA, S.I. (1906–1992)
Canadian-born U.S. senator and educator of Japanese ancestry who became well-known for his work with the science of semantics, the study of the meaning of words. He also served as a college president at San Francisco State University and represented California in the U.S. Senate from 1977–1983.
Books and Reading

HAZLITT, WILLIAM (1778–1830)
English essayist and critic known for his personal essays, in which he expressed his views about great works of literature and the social significance of leading figures of his time.
Friendship and Loyalty, Prejudice

HELLMAN, LILLIAN (1905–1984)
U.S. playwright who was outspoken about social issues of her time. Late in life Hellman wrote several memoirs, including *Scoundrel Time,* which covers the congressional investigations of communist influences in the United States. Her quotation in this book comes from a letter she wrote when the committee asked her, under threat of ending her own career, to name people she knew who may have been communist sympathizers.
Self-Knowledge and Self-Respect

HEMINGWAY, ERNEST (1899–1961)
U.S. author who won both the Nobel Prize in Literature and the Pulitzer Prize. His early novels, including *The Sun Also Rises, A Farewell to Arms,* and *For Whom the Bell Tolls,* grew out of his wartime experiences and stress the need for courage in times of danger as well as when facing the daily challenges of life.
Courage

HENRI IV (HENRY OF NAVARRE) (1553–1610)

King of France who converted to Catholicism to end civil war in his country. He introduced many reforms that improved France's economy and issued the Edict of Nantes, which guaranteed some religious freedom to French Protestants.
Leaders and Leadership

HENRY, MARGUERITE (1902–1997)

U.S. author of Misty books and *King of the Wind,* who became famous for her children's novels about horses.
Animals

HENRY, O. (1862–1910)

U.S. author remembered for his short stories, which often ended with a twist or surprise. His real name was William Sydney Porter and his stories reflected some of the colorful as well as the sadder experiences of his life.
Travel and Adventure, Writing

HENRY, PATRICK (1736–1799)

U.S. Revolutionary leader and governor from Virginia known for his passionate speeches. He argued against the adoption of the Constitution because he was a strong believer in the rights of the states as well as the rights of the individual. He worked to create the Bill of Rights, the first 10 amendments to the Constitution, the purpose of which is to safeguard individual freedoms.
Citizenship and Patriotism, Experience, Freedom, Future, War

HERACLITUS (C. 540–480 B.C.)

Greek philosopher who believed that everything in the world was constantly changing and moving. He lived in Ephesus, a city in what is now part of Turkey.
Change, Character

HERBERT, GEORGE (1593–1633)

British poet who wrote mostly on religious subjects. In 1630 he was ordained as a priest in the Church of England.
Problems and Solutions

HERODOTUS (C. 485–C. 425 B.C.)

Greek historian who wrote nine books about the rise of the Persian Empire, the wars between Persia and Greece, and Greece's victory over Persia after many years of conflict. He traveled widely and studied the culture and history of every place he visited.
Envy and Jealousy

HEYWOOD, JOHN (C. 1497–C. 1580)

British compiler of traditional sayings who in 1546 published a collection called *Proverbs*. This is the earliest collection of English language traditional sayings. He also wrote plays.
Food, Humor, Problems and Solutions

HILLEL (FL. 30 B.C.–A.D. 10)

Jewish religious leader and teacher of ancient Palestine who was one of the most influential and learned spiritual leaders of his time. He founded a school to teach his views and organized the *Talmud,* an important book of

interpretation and commentary on Jewish laws.
Justice and Equality, Right and Wrong**, Self-Knowledge and Self-Respect

HIPPOCRATES (C. 460–377 B.C.)

Greek physician who is known as the "father of medicine" and remembered for his words included under *Health*, which are known as the Hippocratic oath, a promise all doctors take to "do no harm." Although there are many stories about him, little is known about his life, or even if the writings attributed to him are actually his work.
Art, Health

HITLER, ADOLF (1889–1945)

German dictator who is remembered as one of the cruelest, bloodthirsty leaders in world history. He promoted the notion that Germans were an Aryan race and superior to other people. He aggressively attacked other nations, leading to the onset of World War II in Europe. He established concentration camps for Jews, Gypsies, political enemies, and other people he considered "undesirable." The success of the Allies in World War II brought an end to his regime and horrifying policies.
Human Nature

HOCKENBERRY, JOHN (B. 1956)

U.S. journalist who has covered wars all over the world, traveling in his wheelchair. He has won an Emmy and two Peabody awards for his reporting, and told his own story in a book called *Moving Violations*.
Problems and Solutions

HOFFER, ERIC (1902–1983)

U.S. author whose books led to his being known as a political and social philosopher. Before becoming a writer he was as a migrant worker on California farms and a longshoreman.
Manners

HOMER (C. 700 B.C.)

Greek epic poet and storyteller who is famous for composing the *Iliad* and the *Odyssey*. These poems tell the story of the Trojan War and the hero Odysseus, who travels long and far after the war to return to his homeland. The poems were first passed along through the oral tradition, each storyteller changing the poems each time they were told, so many different versions of the stories now exist. After several generations, the poems were copied down and became the basic textbooks used by Greek schoolchildren to learn reading and the legends and myths of their culture.
Citizenship and Patriotism

HOOVER, HERBERT (1874–1964)

Thirty-first president of the United States, who led the country during the early years of the Great Depression, a worldwide failing of the economy in which many people lost their jobs. The American people lost faith in Hoover's leadership because he seemed to act slowly to attack this great problem.
Government and Politics

HORACE (65–8 B.C.)

Roman poet who wrote *Odes,* a collection of short poems about love, friendship, and

nature. He also wrote poetry called *Satires* that poked fun at common human weaknesses.
Advice, Beginnings and Endings, Nature

HOWE, JULIA WARD (1819–1910)
U.S. poet and reformer remembered for writing the words to the patriotic song "The Battle Hymn of the Republic." Her song was popular with the Union troops during the Civil War. She was also known as a popular lecturer who spoke out on cultural topics and such issues as women's rights.
Justice and Equality

HOWELL, JAMES (C. 1594–1666)
British author and historian who published a collection of proverbs in 1659.
Food, Work

HUBBARD, ELBERT (1856–1915)
U.S. printer, editor, and writer who used his publication *The Philistine* to present his own ideas on society and politics.
Science and Technology, Wisdom

HUGHES, LANGSTON (1902–1967)
U.S. poet and author of more than 50 books. This leading member of the Harlem Renaissance used his work to present an African-American perspective. For many years his comic newspaper columns about a character called Jesse B. Simple used humor to make points about human nature and social issues.
Dreams and Goals, Humor

HUGO, VICTOR (1802–1885)
French author who wrote poetry, plays, and novels. A recurring theme in his work is the triumph of the individual spirit despite terrible conditions. Today his novels *Les Miserables* and *The Hunchback of Notre Dame* are still well-known.
Creativity and Ideas, Music

HUIDOBRO, VICENTE (1893–1948)
Chilean poet who lived much his life in Paris and Madrid. He developed a new and experimental form of poetry. Huidobro believed that the poet created a new world, a world better than reality, that grew out of his own imagination.
Introduction, Language and Words

HUNGERFORD, MARGARET (1855–1897)
Irish novelist who wrote *Molly Bawn,* which was published in 1878 and contains the first printed mention of a famous proverb about beauty.
Beauty

HURSTON, ZORA NEALE (C. 1901–1960)
U.S. author and anthropologist who collected black folklore and published short stories, poetry, and essays. She was awarded a Guggenheim Fellowship in 1936 to support her research into the folklore and culture of Jamaica, Haiti, and the African-American South of the U.S. She was perhaps the most prominent female writer in the Harlem Renaissance movement.
Curiosity

HUXLEY, ALDOUS (1894–1963)
British-born author whose novels, including the classic *Brave New World,* helped make him famous. Although his grandfather and brother

were both distinguished biologists, Aldous Huxley used his writing to present his belief that science was destoying people's values.
Apologies and Excuses, Experience

IHARA SAIKAKU (1642–1693)
Japanese author who wrote poetry and novels. He became famous for the speed at which he could compose and recite short poems called haiku. He is reputed to have made up 23,500 haiku in one day.
Wealth and Poverty

INGENIEROS, JOSÉ (1877–1925)
Argentinean philosopher and doctor of psychiatry who studied the workings of the human mind and wrote several books about cultural identity and behavior.
Time

IRVING, WASHINGTON (1783–1859)
U.S. author whose stories, including "The Legend of Sleepy Hollow" and "Rip Van Winkle," drew on the cultural traditions of the Dutch and other European settlers of New York State.
Change, Good Fortune and Misfortune, Greatness

JACKSON, ANDREW (1767–1845)
Seventh president of the United States, who came from Tennessee and who had been a military leader before entering politics. Although he was considered a hero for fighting against the British in the 1815 Battle of New Orleans, he also led raids against the Seminole Indians in Florida and

did little to respect the rights of Native Americans before or after becoming president.
Courage

JACKSON, JESSE (B. 1941)
U.S. minister and politician who sought the democratic nomination for president in 1984 and 1988. He speaks out on issues that concern African-Americans and other people of color throughout the world.
Introduction, Citizenship and Patriotism, Family

JACOBS, HARRIET ANN (1813–1897)
U.S. author who published her personal account of life under slavery. Using the pen name Linda Brent, she published the classic, *Incidents in the Life of a Slave Woman*.
Friendship and Loyalty

JAMES I (1566–1625)
King of England and Scotland who took the English throne in 1603. He encouraged the first English Colonies in America and he commissioned the authorized English language version of the Bible now known as the King James Bible.
News and the Media

JAMES, HENRY (1843–1916)
U.S. author who settled in London and became a British citizen. His novels often contrast the difference between American and British society. He was one of the most influential authors of his time.
Nature

JAMISON, JUDITH (B. 1943)
U.S. dancer and choreographer who began dancing at the age of six. In 1964 she joined

the Alvin Ailey dance company, which features African-American dancers and themes. She assumed directorship of the company after Ailey's death in 1989.
Dance

JEFFERSON, THOMAS (1743–1826)
Third president of the United States, who was highly influential in the development of the new United States of America. He represented Virginia at the Second Continental Congress and was called upon the following year to draft the Declaration of Independence.
Books and Reading, Food, Freedom, Government and Politics**, Justice and Equality, News and the Media

JEWETT, SARAH ORNE (1849–1909)
U.S. author who wrote novels and short stories based on small town life in New England. One of her most famous works is *The Country of The Pointed Firs.*
Friendship and Loyalty

JOHN XXIII, POPE (1881–1963)
Italian-born religious leader who served as the head of the Roman Catholic Church from 1958 until his death. He brought important reforms to the church by promoting cooperation with other religions in the fight against world problems. Born Angelo Giuseppe Roncalli, he became a military chaplain after joining the priesthood. He then went on to serve in the Vatican diplomatic corps and was made a cardinal five years before he was elected pope.
Old Age

JOHNSON, JAMES WELDON (1871–1938)
U.S. poet and songwriter who is remembered for writing the lyrics for the song "Lift Every Voice and Sing." His phrase "Young, Gifted and Black" was also set to music and recorded by Nina Simone and Aretha Franklin, among others. In addition to writing and compiling several collections of poetry, he also wrote fiction and nonfiction about African-American life. Before becoming a writer, he practiced law in Florida and also served as U.S. consul to Nicaragua and Venezuela.
Achievements, Youth

JOHNSON, LYNDON B. (1908–1973)
Thirty-eighth president of the United States, who became president following the fatal shooting of President John F. Kennedy in 1963. Johnson had been Kennedy's vice president and prior to that had served almost 24 years in Congress. He led the nation during the Vietnam War.
Leaders and Leadership, News and the Media, War

JOHNSON, SAMUEL (1709–1784)
British author and compiler of one of the earliest dictionaries of the English language. He is remembered for his dictionary (1755), his wit, and his writings about literature and famous writers.
Community and City Life, Compliments and Insults, Curiosity, Education and Learning, Music

JONES, JAMES EARL (B. 1931)
U.S. actor known for his deep, commanding voice. As a child, he stuttered and was so self-conscious that he rarely spoke. However, he went on to study acting in college, and in

1969 he received a Tony Award for his performance in *The Great White Hope*, a play based on the life of a great African-American boxer. Since then he has starred on the stage and in films, and in 1992 he was awarded the National Medal for the Arts.
Achievements

JONES, MOTHER (1830–1930)
U.S. labor leader who was born in Ireland and came to the U.S. as a child. She helped organize unions, first in the coal mines of Pennsylvania, West Virginia, and Colorado, and later among garment workers in New York City. Her fiery speeches inspired many workers to strike and in other ways take action to obtain better working conditions. Her full name was Mary Harris Jones.
Action

JORDAN, MICHAEL (B. 1963)
U.S. basketball player who has been named Most Valuable Player by the National Basketball Association. This Chicago Bulls star also represented the U.S. as a member of the "Dream Team" in the Olympics in 1992 and 1996.
Sports

JOSEPH, CHIEF (HINMATON YALAKTIT) (C. 1840–1904)
Nez Perce chief who attempted to lead his people to Canada to avoid forced resettlement on a reservation.
Freedom, Truth and Reality, Justice and Equality

JOUBERT, JOSEPH (1754–1824)
French essayist who wrote on moral issues. His writings were collected in a book called *Pensées* (*Thoughts*) in 1838.
Education and Learning

JUVENAL (A.D. C. 55–130)
Roman author known for his satires, humorous works that he used to poke fun at the flaws he saw in people and society. In his tenth satire he urges readers not to seek power or wealth but instead to wish for a "sound mind in a sound body."
Health

KAHLO, FRIDA (1907–1954)
Mexican painter known for her self-portraits, in which she used unusual symbols to reveal her thoughts about her life. She was married to another famous Mexican painter, Diego Rivera. In 1985 the Mexican government declared her paintings national treasures.
*Art***

KANUDA, KENNETH (B. 1924)
Zambian politician who helped his country achieve independence in 1964 and served as the first president of Zambia.
Justice and Equality

KARR, ALPHONSE (1808–1890)
French journalist who edited *Figaro* and founded and wrote his famous quote in *Les Guépes,* a review that presented satires that mocked different aspects of society.
Change

KAYYÁM, OMAR SEE OMAR KAYYÁM

KEATS, JOHN (1795–1821)

British poet who often used his poetry to celebrate beauty found in nature and art. His famous quotes on beauty come from a long poem called *Endymion* (1818) and "Ode to a Grecian Urn"(1828). In the second poem, the poet has the urn itself speak about the relationship between beauty and truth.
Beauty, Experience

KELLER, HELEN (1880–1968)

U.S. author and advocate for the disabled who became blind and deaf when she suffered a severe illness at the age of nineteen months. Her determined mother found a teacher, Anne Sullivan, who began to educate Helen in 1887. Helen Keller learned to sign and speak as well as to read Braille. She authored several books and lectured on behalf of the disabled.
Books and Reading

KENNEDY, JOHN FITZGERALD (1917–1963)

Thirty-fifth president of the United States, who was the youngest man and the first Roman Catholic ever elected to that office. He became the youngest to die in office when he was killed by an assassin's bullet. He wrote several books and served in the Senate before becoming president. His famous quote on citizenship comes from his first inaugural address (1961).
Citizenship and Patriotism, Creativity and Ideas, Success

KENNEDY, ROBERT (1925–1968)

U.S. Senator and attorney general who was the brother of President John F. Kennedy. He worked actively for civil rights. He was assassinated while campaigning for the Democratic nomination for president.
Prejudice

KENNEDY, X. J. (B. 1929)

U.S. poet whose collections of poems for children include *One Winter Night in August* and *The Forgetful Wishing Well.* His poetry is known for his playful use of language and inventive comparisons. His real name is Joseph Charles Kennedy.
Animals

KENNER, BEATRICE (B. 1912)

U.S. inventor who holds more patents for new inventions than any other African-American woman. Her inventions focus on little everyday things that make life easier for ordinary people.
Science and Technology

KENNY, SISTER ELIZABETH (1880–1952)

Australian nurse who developed a technique for helping polio victims reeducate their muscles. Before there was a vaccine to prevent this illness, many people were left paralyzed from its effects.
Courage

KERR, JEAN (B. 1923)

U.S. author whose humorous works about everyday life include *Please Don't Eat the Daisies.*
Introduction

KETTERING, CHARLES F. (1876–1958)

U.S. scientist who trained as an electrical engineer. He developed the first electric cash

register and worked on improving automobiles for General Motors. His inventions made him a wealthy man, and he donated funds to establish important research; he was cofounder of the Sloan-Kettering Institute for Cancer Research.
Future

KHAN, GENGHIS SEE **GENGHIS** KHAN

KIERKEGAARD, SÖREN (1813–1855)
Danish philosopher and religious thinker who wrote a great deal about his religious beliefs and the effect having faith has on an individual.
Self-Knowledge and Self-Respect

KILMER, JOYCE (1886–1918)
U.S. poet who wrote many poems, but is primarily remembered for one: "Trees" (1913). His full name was Alfred Joyce Kilmer.
Nature

KING, MARTIN LUTHER, JR. (1929–1968)
U.S. minister and civil rights leader who began his career as pastor of a Baptist church. He believed in nonviolent protest against injustice and used these techniques to organize boycotts and demonstrations to fight racial discrimination.
*Courage and Unity, Dreams and Goals**, Government and Politics, Right and Wrong*

KIPLING, RUDYARD (1865–1936)
British author who was born in India and later returned there as a young journalist. He began writing stories inspired by local events. Many of his later and more famous stories and poems, including *The Jungle Book* and *Kim*, were also inspired by his time in India. In 1907 Kipling became the first English author to win the Nobel Prize in Literature.
Introduction, Travel and Adventure

KORMAN, GORDON (B. 1963)
Canadian author known for his humorous novels about school life in Canada and the U.S. He wrote and published his first novel about his now popular characters Boots and Bruno when he was a young teenager.
Youth

KUHN, MAGGIE (1905–1995)
U.S. civil rights activist who founded a group called the Gray Panthers. She wrote and spoke eloquently about the contributions older citizens could and do make to society, and fought against discrimination based on age.
Old Age

LA FOLLETTE, SUZANNE (1893–1983)
U.S. politician and writer who was known for her work for women's rights.
Youth

LA FONTAINE, JEAN DE (1621–1695)
French poet and fable writer. His *Fables* consist of 240 short stories with morals, all told in verse. Modeled after Aesop's *Fables*, these poems use many animal characters to tell stories that teach lessons about human behavior.
Work

LAO-TZU (C. 604–531 B.C.)
Chinese philosopher credited with developing Taoism and author of the *Tao Te Ching*, a

classic manual on the art of living a good life. After the Bible, the *Tao Te Ching* is the most translated book in world literature. Little is known about the life of Lao-tzu. Some modern scholars believe that the *Tao Te Ching*, although credited to him, may have actually been the work of many authors.
Beauty, Beginnings and Endings, Courage, Education and Learning, Leaders and Leadership

LEACOCK, STEPHEN (1869–1944)
Canadian humorist and economist better known by most readers for his humorous publications than his scholarly works. Most of his humorous writings first appeared in magazines and newspapers and were later collected into books.
Good Fortune and Misfortune

LE CORBUSIER (1887–1965)
Swiss-born French architect and city planner whose real name was Charles Édouard Jeanneret. He opened a studio in Paris in 1922 and there developed the idea of tall apartment buildings surrounded by green spaces.
Home

LEE, ROBERT E. (1807–1870)
U.S. military leader and commander of the Confederate Army during the Civil War. Lee graduated from the U.S. Military Academy at West Point and served in the U.S. Army until 1861, when he resigned out of loyalty to his home state of Virginia. When he assumed command of the Confederate forces, he knew his resources were no match for the Union Army. He is credited with leading a brilliant defensive operation until he surrendered to General Ulysses S. Grant in 1865.
War

L'ENGLE, MADELINE (B. 1918)
U.S. author known for her novels for children and adults. She won the Newbery Award in 1963 for her science-fiction classic *A Wrinkle in Time.*
Choices

LEONARDO DA VINCI (1452–1519)
Italian artist and inventor who kept detailed notebooks in which he recorded his observations about nature and people and drew plans for hundreds of inventions including a flying machine. His famous paintings include the *Mona Lisa* and *The Last Supper.*
Compliments and Insults, Friendship and Loyalty, Love and Hate, Science and Technology

LEVENSON, SAM (1911–1980)
U.S. humorist known for writing about the funny things that happen in everyday family life.
Youth

LÉVI-STRAUSS, CLAUDE (B. 1908)
French anthropologist who was born in Belgium and studied at the University of Paris. He became famous for his application of a method of analysis called Structuralism which he used in studies of family relationships and the myths found in different cultures.
Science and Technology

LÉVIS, GASTON PIERRE MARC, DUC DE (1764–1830)
French nobleman who included his now-famous quotation about the obligations of the nobility in his *Maxims and Reflections* (1808).
Responsibility

LEWIS, C. S. (1898–1963)
British author whose full name was Clive Staples Lewis. He wrote more than 30 books, including science fiction and religious works. From 1950–1956 he wrote the well-loved series of children's books called The Chronicles of Narnia.
Future

LIN, MAYA (B. 1959)
U.S. architect of Chinese descent who designed the Vietnam War Memorial in Washington, D. C. She was a student in architecture school when she submitted her design for the memorial.
War

LIN YUTANG (1895–1976)
Chinese-American author who was born in China but lived mostly in the U.S. from 1936–1966. He wrote both in Chinese and English. His books helped Westerners learn about Chinese culture.
Ability and Talent

LINCOLN, ABRAHAM (1809–1865)
Sixteenth president of the United States, who led the country through the Civil War. Before and during his presidency, Lincoln gave speeches and wrote letters that include some of the most famous lines from American history. His first inaugural address (1861) and the Gettysburg Address (1863) are among the speeches he wrote in his efforts to bring the nation together. On less formal occasions, Lincoln was also known for his sense of humor. He poked fun at his own looks and political life. At home he was a devoted father, sometimes criticized for spoiling his children.
Introduction, Advice, Beauty, Dreams and Goals, Family, Freedom, Future, Government and Politics, Self-Knowledge and Self-Respect, Truth and Reality

LINDBERGH, ANNE MORROW (B. 1906)
U.S. essayist and aviator whose life was marked by both great adventure and accomplishment. She was a licensed pilot and made many long trips with her husband, aviator Charles Lindbergh. She wrote several books about her travels as well as the popular book *Gifts from the Sea*. However, her life also included great tragedy; in 1932 her infant son was kidnapped and killed.
Travel and Adventure

LINNAEUS, CAROLUS (CARL VON LINNÉ) (1707–1778)
Swedish scientist who specialized in the study of plants. He also established the modern scientific system for classifying and naming plants and animals. He traveled widely in his studies. In 1842 he became a professor of botany at the University of Upsala.
Education and Learning, Nature

LIVY (59 B.C.–A.D. 17)

Roman historian who wrote a 142-book history of Rome. He spent more than 40 years working on his history.
Time

LOCKE, JOHN (1632–1704)

British philosopher whose book *Two Treatises of Government* (1690) and essay *Concerning Human Understanding* (1690) presented ideas that influenced Thomas Jefferson and others who helped found the United States. Locke believed that all people were entitled to liberty and political equality.
Change, Government and Politics

LOMBARDI, VINCE (1913–1970)

U.S. football coach who was voted into the Pro Football Hall of Fame in 1971. As head coach for the Green Bay Packers, he stressed team pride, hard work, and determination. Under his leadership, his team won five NFL championships and two Super Bowls. In 1969 he became part owner and head coach of the Washington Redskins.
Sports

LONE MAN (ISNA LA-WICA) (C. LATE 19TH CENTURY)

Teton Sioux leader whose people lived in what is now North and South Dakota. The name Teton (Tituniwan) means "people of the prairie."
Cooperation and Unity

LONGFELLOW, HENRY WADSWORTH (1807–1882)

U.S. poet who often wrote about American history and the sea. His most famous poems include "The Song of Hiawatha" and "Paul Revere's Ride." In his poem "My Lost Youth," quoted in this book, he adapted the lines from an old Lapland song.
Action, Apologies and Excuses, Greatness, Music, Problems and Solutions, Success, Wisdom, Youth

LOPEZ, NANCY (B. 1957)

U.S. golfer who won her first championship at the age of nine and who, by the age of twelve, was defeating professional adult women golfers. At the age of sixteen she was ranked first among amateur woman golfers. She became a professional golfer in 1978 and soon became the first to win five Ladies Professional Golf Association tournaments in a row. In 1987 she was elected into the Ladies Professional Golf Association Hall of Fame.
Sports

LU HSÜN (OR LU XUN) (1881–1936)

Chinese writer whose real name was Chou Shu-jen. He was considered the greatest writer of his time and pioneered a new, more realistic style of writing, using everyday words rather than classic phrases as had been typical of earlier Chinese writers.
Time

LUCE, CLAIRE BOOTHE (1903–1987)

U.S. author and diplomat who was awarded the Presidential Medal of Freedom in 1983. She served in the U.S. Congress and as an

ambassador to Brazil. Earlier in her career she worked as a journalist and won acclaim as a playwright.
Courage, Helping and Kindness

LUTHER, MARTIN (1483–1546)
German religious leader and reformer who founded the Protestant Reformation. He also translated the Bible into German and wrote many hymns.
Justice and Equality

MA, YO-YO (B. 1955)
French-born U.S. cellist of Chinese descent. He is a popular performer of classical music and has given concerts all over the world.
Music

MACARTHUR, GENERAL DOUGLAS (1880–1964)
U.S. military leader who led troops in both World War I and World War II. He was appointed Commander of the Allied Forces in the Southwest Pacific and led these forces to victory over the Japanese. However, in 1950 when he again led troops during the Korean War, he clashed with President Truman and was dismissed for wanting to extend the war into China.
War

MACHIAVELLI, NICCOLÒ (1469–1527)
Italian statesman and philosopher whose most famous work is *The Prince* (1513), which presents his theories on how a leader should govern. He based his philosophy on his own experiences in politics and on his study of

history. He believed a leader was justified in using anything, even cruelty and lies, to reach his or her goals.
Love and Hate, War

MAISTRE, JOSEPH MARIE, COMTE DE (1753–1821)
French philosopher who believed strongly that the church and king should have absolute power. He opposed the French Revolution.
Government and Politics

MALCOLM X (1925–1965)
Minister of the Nation of Islam and U.S. civil rights leader who went to prison for robbery when he was twenty-one. In prison he was exposed to the Black Muslim faith. He converted, changing his name from Malcolm Little to Malcolm X. After his release from prison he became one of the Nation of Islam's most eloquent ministers, spreading the messages of pride in race and separatism. In 1963 he founded the Organization for Afro-America Unity, converted to orthodox Islam, softened his separatist views, and worked for social reforms. He was killed by an assassin's bullet, and his autobiography was completed by Alex Haley and published after his death.
Advice, Books and Reading, Mathematics

MANDELA, NELSON (B. 1918)
President of South Africa who devoted many years to fighting apartheid (separation of the races) in his homeland. In 1964 he was sentenced to life in prison for his role in leading Black South Africans to speak out for their rights. His courage and commitment

inspired many South Africans and others around the world to demand an end to apartheid, and many reforms became law. Mandela was released from prison in 1990. In 1994 he was elected president.
Character

MANN, HORACE (1796–1859)
U.S. educator who fought for educational reforms that would allow children all over the country to attend public elementary schools.
Education and Learning

MANN, THOMAS (1875–1955)
German author who became famous for his novels and won the Nobel Prize in Literature in 1929.
Creativity and Ideas

MARCUS AURELIUS (121–A.D. 180)
Roman emperor and philosopher who believed that all people are citizens of the earth and should help each other.
Community and City Life, Time

MARIE ANTOINETTE (1755–1793)
Queen of France who influenced her husband, King Louis XVI, to refuse to reform the government to give the common people more rights. After the Revolutionary forces gained control, she was condemned to death by the Revolutionary Tribunal and guillotined.
Food

MARQUIS, DON (1878–1937)
U.S. humorist and journalist who published a column in the *New York Sun*. In his column he wrote about the adventures of a cat named

mehetabel and a cockroach named archy. Everything about these animals was written in lower case letters because Marquis presented the stories as if archy had written them by jumping from key to key on a typewriter.
Cooperation and Unity

MARTI, JOSÉ (1853–1895)
Cuban patriot and poet whose full name was José Julian Marti y Perez. He actively fought for Cuba's independence from Spain. Many of his poems speak of freedom. He also wrote essays on many subjects, including people he admired, such as Ralph Waldo Emerson, Walt Whitman, and Simón Bolívar.
Leaders and Leadership

MARTIAL (A.D. C. 40–C. 104)
Spanish-born Roman author who wrote many poems and collections of wise and clever sayings (epigrams) told in rhyme.
Greatness

MARTIN, JUDITH ("MISS MANNERS") (B. 1938)
U.S. humorist and authority on manners whose books include *Miss Manners' Guide to Rearing Perfect Children* (1984) and *Miss Manners' Guide for the Turn of the Millennium* (1989).
Manners

MARX, GROUCHO (1895–1977)
U.S. humorist and film star whose real name was Julius Henry Marx. Along with his siblings, he became famous as part of a comedy team called the Marx Brothers.

Groucho later went on to star as the host of a popular television game show.
Apologies and Excuses, Compliments and Insults, News and the Media

MAYER, MARIA GOEPPERT (1906–1972)
German-born U.S. physicist who shared the Nobel Prize in Physics in 1930 with two other scientists for her work on the structure of the nucleus of the atom.
Science and Technology

McAULIFFE, CHRISTA (1948–1986)
U.S. high school social studies teacher who was selected from over 11,000 applicants to be the first schoolteacher to travel into space. Tragically, the space shuttle *Challenger*, on which she was to make this historic flight, exploded shortly after takeoff, resulting in the death of McAuliffe and the six other astronauts aboard.
Education and Learning

McLUHAN, MARSHALL (1911–1980)
Canadian educator and media theorist who became famous for his ideas about how the kinds of technology people use to communicate change the way they think and behave.
Community and City Life, News and the Media, Youth

McCLUNG, NELLIE (1873–1951)
Canadian politician and advocate for women's rights who served in the Alberta legislature. She was one of several women who went to court in 1927 to prove that women were "persons" and therefore had full rights under the British North American Act (the Canadian constitution). She also wrote several books about Canadian life and the women's movement.
Justice and Equality

MEAD, MARGARET (1901–1978)
U.S. anthropologist who became famous for her books about the time she spent studying tribal cultures in Samoa, New Guinea, Bali, and other places. She believed that culture influences people's personalities as well as their behavior.
Change

MELVILLE, HERMAN (1819–1891)
U.S. author who spent part of his childhood at sea as a cabin boy and part of his adulthood as a seaman aboard whaling ships. His life experiences inspired many of the books he wrote, including the now classic *Moby Dick*.
Greatness

MENCIUS (MENG-TZU) (372–289 B.C.)
Chinese philosopher who was the grandson of Confucius. He taught his own system for ethical behavior and served as a political advisor for several Chinese rulers. His teachings were collected by his disciples into a book called *Meng-tzu*. When his book became known in other lands, his name was often written in Latinized form as Mencius.
Greatness

MERRITT, DIXON LANIER (1879–1972)
U.S. poet whose humorous work "The Pelican" (1910) is often quoted today.
Animals

MERTON, THOMAS (1915–1968)
French-born U.S. Trappist priest and author whose most famous works include *No Man is an Island* and *Thoughts in Solitude*.
Right and Wrong

MICHELANGELO (1475–1564)
Italian artist known for his sculpture, paintings, architecture, and poetry. He is remembered as one of the greatest artists who ever lived. His famous works reflect mostly religious themes and include the fresco painted on the ceiling of the Sistine Chapel in the Vatican in 1511 and his statue of *David*. His full name was Michelangelo Buonarroti.
Art

MIES VAN DER ROHE, LUDWIG (1886–1969)
German architect known for his furniture, office buildings, and apartment houses, which featured very simple designs.
Art

MILL, JOHN STUART (1806–1873)
British philosopher who wrote about methods for applying logical reasoning, economic theory and politics, and the rights of women. When he was three, his father began his education, teaching him according to the theory of utilitarianism, which stresses that whatever brings the greatest good to the greatest number of people is the best course to follow.
Education and Learning

MILLAY, EDNA ST. VINCENT (1892–1950)
U.S. poet who won the Pulitzer Prize in poetry in 1923. Critics consider many of the poems she wrote early in her career to be among her best works, especially those that deal with love and the enthusiasm and rebelliousness of youth.
Effort and Enthusiasm

MILLER, ARTHUR (B. 1915)
U.S. playwright who won a Pulitzer Prize for his play *Death of a Salesman* (1949). His other famous works include *The Crucible* (1953).
News and the Media

MITCHELL, MARIA (1818–1889)
U.S. astronomer and educator who in 1847 established the orbit of a newly discovered comet and became the first woman elected to the American Academy of Arts and Sciences. She later taught astronomy at Vassar College in Poughkeepsie, New York.
Nature, Self-Knowledge and Self-Respect, Travel and Adventure

MOHAMMAD SEE MUHAMMAD

MOLIÈRE (1622–1673)
French playwright whose real name was Jean Baptiste Poquelin. He began as an actor and formed his own troupe, known as the King's Comedians. He wrote comedies for his own troupe to perform, but his works, considered to be among the finest plays ever written in French, are still performed and read today.
Food, Writing

MOMADAY, N. SCOTT (B. 1934)

Kiowa author and professor of literature and Native American studies whose writing draws from Native Amercian culture and his family experiences. His works include *House Made of Dawn* (1964), for which he won the Pulitzer Prize, and *The Way to Rainy Mountain* (1969). He is also known by the name Tsaoi-talee (Rock tree boy).
Nature

MONET, CLAUDE (1840–1926)

French painter who was a leader in the Impressionist movement. He was especially concerned with the way light was depicted when he painted outdoor scenes. Among his most famous works are a series of paintings of waterlilies, inspired by the pond and flowers in his own garden in Giverny.
Art

MONROE, JAMES (1758–1831)

Fifth president of the United States, who as president enacted the Monroe Doctrine (1823), which warned European nations not to interfere with the free nations of the Western Hemisphere.
Citizenship and Patriotism, Government and Politics

MONTAGU, LADY MARY WORTLEY (1689–1762)

British poet also known for her letter writing and for being a leader of society and fashion trends. Her friends included authors Jonathan Swift and Alexander Pope.
Manners

MONTAIGNE, MICHEL DE (1533–1592)

French lawyer and essayist who is credited as being the first person to write personal essays. He developed this form when he became ill and mistakenly thought he would soon die. He wanted to leave behind his impressions and opinions on many subjects as part of his legacy to his family and friends. He is sometimes referred to as Michel Eyquem de Montaigne.
Animals, Human Nature, Language and Words

MONTGOMERY, LUCY MAUD (1874–1942)

Canadian author of the classic *Anne of Green Gables* and a number of other books about this spirited young heroine. Montgomery based many of her stories on her own childhood on Prince Edward Island.
Writing

MOORE, GEORGE (1852–1933)

Irish author who published works of poetry, short stories, and novels. He studied art in Paris with some of the greatest artists of the time, but then discovered that he preferred writing to painting. In 1901, after a number of years abroad, he returned home to Ireland.
Home

MORGAN, JOHN PIERPONT (1837–1913)

U.S. banker and financier who helped organize the United States Steel Corporation and served as a director of many leading corporations, banks, railroads, and public utilities. His great wealth and associations with so many important companies made him one of the most powerful people of his time.
Problems and Solutions

MOTHER GOOSE SEE GOOSE, MOTHER

MOTHER TERESA SEE TERESA, MOTHER

MOURNING DOVE (CHRISTINE QUINTASKET) (C. 1885–1936)
Okanagan Salish author who in 1927 published a novel *Co-Ge-We-A*, one of the first novels ever published by a Native American author.
Faith and Hope

MOYERS, BILL (B. 1934)
U.S. television journalist who is known for his programs on public television and the best-selling books based on some of his shows, including *A World of Ideas* and *Genesis.*
News and the Media

MUHAMMAD (C. 570–632)
Prophet of Islam who founded this religion. Around 610 he began having prophetic visions and revelations, 650 of which were written down to become the Koran, the most sacred book of Islam. Muslims believe that Muhammad was the last messenger of God. The name Muhammad means "praised one."
Action, Creativity and Ideas, Education and Learning, Helping and Kindness, Right and Wrong

MUIR, JOHN (1838 –1914)
Scottish-born U.S. naturalist who traveled across the United States and many other lands camping and exploring nature. He kept a diary of his observations and thoughts and published several books based on his travels. On a special camping trip, he convinced President Theodore Roosevelt to set aside 148,000,000 acres of forest reserves.
Nature

MULRONEY, BRIAN (B. 1939)
Canadian prime minister elected in 1984. During his time in office, Canada faced a Constitutional crisis when many people from the Province of Quebec urged the government to accept Quebec as an independent state. Mulroney set up a commission and enacted new programs with the goal of promoting national unity.
Government and Politics

MURDOCH, IRIS (B. 1919)
Irish-born British author known for her novels. Her full name is Jean Iris Murdoch, and in addition to writing she taught philosophy at Oxford University from 1948–1963. In recognition for her contributions as a novelist, she was made Dame Commander of the Order of the British Empire in 1987.
Travel and Aventure

MURPHY'S LAW
Some scholars believe that what we now refer to as Murphy's Law is an old, anonymous saying. However, it is called Murphy's Law because in 1949, George Nichols, a U.S. aerospace executive, credited Captain E. Murphey with saying these words. The press was covering Nichols's remarks and Murphy's Law became a popular saying. (The spelling of Murphey's name got changed along the way.)
Problems and Solutions

NĀLĀDIYAR-DIVYA

This book of ethical teachings represents the work of 12 Tamil poet-saints and was written between the years 650–940. Its name means "4,000 Divine Verses." The Tamil-speaking people originated and continue to live in the south of India in a an area now known as Tamil Nadu. However, millions of Tamil people now live throughout the rest of the world.
Education and Learning

NAPOLEON I (1769–1821)

French general and emperor whose full name was Napoleon Bonaparte. He built an empire that covered most of western and central Europe. He was only 5'2' tall, shorter than most other men of his day, but he was an inspiring and demanding leader, one who was also known for his great ambition.
Food, News and the Media, War

NASH, OGDEN (1902–1971)

U.S. humorist and poet whose full name was Frederic Ogden Nash. Many of his funny poems appeared in *The New Yorker* magazine. Several collections of his poems were also published in book form.
Animals

NAVRATILOVA, MARTINA (B. 1956)

Czech-born U.S. tennis champion known for her strong serve and powerful and aggressive style of playing the game. Her mother had been a ski instructor and her grandmother a tennis player, and their examples inspired Navratilova's love of sports. Championships she has won include Wimbeldon (nine times) and the U.S. Open.
Sports

NERO (A.D. 37–68)

Roman emperor who ruled from A.D. 54 until his death. He committed suicide rather than face the wrath of his military commanders, who had begun to revolt against him. He considered himself an artist because at times he acted in plays, wrote poetry, and also was interested in architecture. However, he is also remembered for his cruelty. Rumors say that he caused a fire that burned down much of Rome so he could build himself a new palace. Then he blamed the Christians for the blaze, beginning the Roman persecution of this religious group.
Confidence

NEWTON, SIR ISAAC (1642–1727)

British scientist and mathematician who developed theories about motion and gravity. He changed how scientists thought of the way the planets move through the heavens as well as the way objects move on earth.
Ability and Talent, Science and Technology

NKRUMAH, KWAME (1909–1972)

President of Ghana (1960–1966) who was a key figure in liberating his homeland from British rule. In 1966, while Nkrumah was on a state visit to China, military leaders took over Ghana's government, forcing him into exile in nearby Guinea.
Government and Politics

NORTON, THOMAS (1532–1584)
British lawyer and poet who was also known for his skill as a debater in Parliament.
Faith and Hope

O'CASEY, SEAN (1880–1964)
Irish playwright who became famous for the plays he wrote for the Abbey Theatre in Dublin about Irish working-class life. He also wrote a six-volume autobiography, *Mirror in My House.*
Old Age

OKARA, GABRIEL (B. 1921)
Nigerian writer who has written poetry, novels, and short stories. He is best known for his poetry and for his skill in capturing African speech patterns in English. He is also known by the name Imomotimi Gbaingbain.
Language and Words

O'KEEFFE, GEORGIA (1887–1986)
U.S. painter who is considered one of the most important American artists of the 20th century. Flowers, animal bones, and rocks are displayed in many of her paintings, inspired by her experiences in the desert of New Mexico.
Experience

OLMEDO, JOSÉ JOAQUIN DE (1780–1847)
Ecuadorian poet who devoted his life to his nation's winning its freedom from Spain. He is best known for a poem he wrote in praise of freedom fighter Simón Bolívar.
Faith and Hope

OMAR KHAYYÁM (C. 1048–C. 1131)
Persian poet, mathematician, astronomer and philosopher. Best known for the *Rubiyat*, a collection of poems in which each poem is four lines long and the 1st, 2nd, and 4th lines rhyme. His *Rubiyat* was translated into English by the British poet Edward FitzGerald in 1859.
Future

ONIZUKA, ELLISON (1946–1986)
U.S. astronaut of Japanese descent who was one of the seven crew members who died tragically when the space shuttle *Challenger* exploded shortly after its launch.
Responsibility

OROZCO, JOSÉ CLEMENTE (1883–1949)
Mexican painter who is remembered for his murals, which depict events from Mexican history and cultural traditions.
Creativity and Ideas

PACHACUTEC INCA YUPANQUI (1438–1471)
Incan ruler who extended his empire to what is now southern Peru and to Ecuador.
Courage, Envy and Jealousy

PAIGE, SATCHEL (C. 1906–1982)
U.S. baseball player known for his great pitching in the Negro Leagues (1924–47). He became the first African-American pitcher in the American League in 1948. In 1971 he was elected to the Baseball Hall of Fame. His real name was Leroy Robert Paige.
Old Age

PARKER, CHARLIE (1920–1955)
U.S. jazz saxophonist known for his ability to make up (improvise) music as he performed on the alto sax. His nickname was "Bird" and his full name was Charles Christopher Parker.
Music

PARKS, ROSA (B. 1913)
U.S. civil rights leader who became famous in 1955 when she refused to give up her seat on a Montgomery, Alabama, bus so that a white man could sit down. At that time a city law said that white people and black people had to sit in separate rows, with far more seats in better locations reserved for whites. As an NAACP organizer she worked then and continues to work for social reform and the rights of African-Americans.
Prejudice

PASTEUR, LOUIS (1822–1895)
French scientist who, through careful experimentation, discovered that some diseases are spread by bacteria. He developed a process called pasteurization that uses heat to kill bacteria in milk and other foods. He also developed vaccines to protect people and animals against diseases.
Science and Technology

PATERSON, KATHERINE (B. 1932)
U.S. author of *A Bridge to Terabithia* and many other award-winning books for young readers. In 1988 she was awarded the Regina medal for her lifetime contribution to children's literature.
Writing

PAYNE, JOHN HOWARD (1791–1852)
U.S. actor, playwright, and lyricist who is remembered for his song "Home, Sweet Home." He wrote this song for his opera *Clari, the Maid of Milan* (1823).
Home

PAZ, OCTAVIO (B. 1914)
Mexican author who won the 1990 Nobel Prize in Literature. His poetry and essays reflect his interest in Mexican history and civilization as well as politics. From 1962 to 1968 he served as Mexico's ambassador to India.
Creativity and Ideas, Government and Politics

PECK, ANNIE SMITH (1850–1935)
U.S. pioneering mountain climber who in 1908, at the age of fifty-seven, became the first person to climb the 21,812-foot peak of Mount Huascaran in the Peruvian Andes. She began climbing mountains in 1885 and went on to scale peaks in the Swiss Alps, Mexico, and the U.S. When she was eighty-two, she made her last climb on Mount Madison in New Hampshire.
Sports

PICASSO, PABLO (1881–1973)
Spanish painter and sculptor whose full name was Pablo Ruiz y Picasso. During his lifetime he created over 20,000 works of art, including paintings, sculpture, prints, and ceramics. He was one of the most influential artists of the 20th century.
Animals, Art

PIGGY, MISS (CREATED 1980)

Muppet television personality created by Jim Henson and Frank Oz. She is known for her affection for Kermit the Frog, her belief in her own talent and beauty, and her healthy appetite.
Food

PICKENS, WILLIAM (1881–1954)

U.S. educator and civil rights leader who served for more than 20 years as a field secretary for the NAACP (National Association for the Advancement of Colored People). He also served as dean of Morgan State University. He wrote many essays and articles and published his autobiography, *Bursting Bounds,* in 1923.
Action

PIPPIN, HORACE (1888–1946)

U.S. painter who was self-taught. His right arm was paralyzed due to an injury he received in World War I, and he worked at a variety of jobs throughout his life. Late in life he became well-known for his artwork depicting African-American culture.
Art

PLATO (C. 428–348 B.C.)

Greek philosopher who was a pupil of Socrates and the teacher of Aristotle. His early *Dialogues* record the teachings of Socrates. His later writings include *The Republic* and present his own ideas about nature, politics, education, art, and the human soul. He

believed in the importance of order and harmony in all things.
Achievements, Beginnings and Endings, Dance, Problems and Solutions

PLAUTUS, TITUS MACCIUS (C. 254–184 B.C.)

Roman playwright known for his comedies. He wrote 21 plays and had worked as a stagehand and actor before he began to write.
Action

PLINY THE ELDER (A.D. 23–79)

Roman scholar and naturalist who served as a cavalry commander and wrote and studied many subjects, including military strategies, history, and science. He died while trying to help people escape from Pompeii when Mount Vesuvius erupted. He is remembered as Pliny the Elder because his nephew, Pliny the Younger, was also a famous writer.
Home

PLUTARCH (A.D. 46–120)

Greek biographer who became famous for his book *Parallel Lives of Illustrious Greeks and Romans*. This book, commonly known as *Plutarch's Lives*, pairs famous Greeks and Romans and gives important historical information about their lives and times. Plutarch spent years traveling through Greece, Italy, and Egypt collecting facts for his book. He was also a priest of Apollo at Delphi.
Greatness

POE, EDGAR ALLAN (1809–1849)

U.S. author known for his chillingly suspenseful stories and dramatic, rhythmic

poetry. His story "The Murders in the Rue Morgue" is considered to be one of the first modern detective stories. His other famous works include "The Tell-Tale Heart" and "The Pit and the Pendulum" and the poems "The Raven" and "Annabel Lee."
Truth and Reality

POPE, ALEXANDER (1688–1744)
British author known for his poetry that exposed the foolish things that people do as part of their everyday lives. He wrote his poems by stringing together heroic couplets, two rhymed lines of 10 syllables each. His famous couplet about hope comes from a long poem called *An Essay on Man*. He was also known for his clever letter writing and conversation. Because of an illness he suffered at the age of twelve, Pope had a spinal deformity and never grew taller than 4′6″; throughout his life he remained extremely sensitive about his appearance.
Education and Learning, Faith and Hope, Human Nature

POPEYE (CREATED 1929)
Cartoon character who usually saves the day after eating a can of spinach. He made his first appearance in a comic strip called *Thimble Theater* written and drawn by E. C. Segar. Popeye went on to star in animated cartoons shown in the movies and later on television.
Food

PORTER, WILLIAM SYDNEY SEE
O. HENRY

POWELL, COLIN (B. 1937)
U.S. military leader who served as Chairman of the Joint Chiefs of Staff, the principal military advisor to the president of the U.S. He was named to that post by President George Bush in 1989. In 1991 Powell oversaw Operation Desert Storm when U.S. troops and troops from other nations invaded Iraq.
Leaders and Leadership

PRESCOTT, WILLIAM (1726–1795)
American Revolutionary soldier who fought at the Battle of Bunker Hill. He commanded a regiment of Minutemen in the earliest days of the Revolutionary War.
*War***

PRICE, LEONTYNE (B. 1927)
U.S. opera singer who made history in 1960 when she sang the title role in the opera *Aida* in the La Scala opera house in Milan, Italy. She was the first woman of African descent to play a leading role there. Aida remained one of her favorite roles, but she also performed the leading soprano roles in many other operas. She received the Presidential Medal of Freedom in 1964.
Self-Knowledge and Self-Respect

PROVERBS, TRADITIONAL SAYINGS, AND SONGS

African-American
Good Fortune and Misfortune, Justice and Equality

Algerian
Travel and Adventure

American
*Confidence, Curiosity, Education and Learning**,
Envy and Jealousy, Food**, Greatness, Health,
Justice and Equality, Right and Wrong, Success,
Truth and Reality**, Youth*

Arab
*Beauty, Envy and Jealousy, Faith and Hope,
Helping and Kindness, Humor, Justice and
Equality*

Armenian
Truth and Reality

Ashanti (African)
Good Fortune and Misfortune, Peace

Bambara (African)
Apologies and Excuses

Baptist hymn
Faith and Hope

Benin (African)
Community and City Life

Chinese
*Ability and Talent, Books and Reading, Character,
Experience, Happiness and Sorrow, Helping and
Kindness, Human Nature, Leaders and Leadership,
Sports, Wisdom*

Chippewa (Ojibwa)
Happiness and Sorrow, Music

Congo (African)
Truth and Reality**

Costa Rican
Experience

Cuban
Happiness and Sorrow

Djuka (African)
Character

Dutch
Right and Wrong

Ecuadorian
Helping and Kindness

Egyptian
Manners

English
*Animals**, Beginnings and Endings, Food**,
Good Fortune and Misfortune, Justice and
Equality, Manners, Problems and Solutions, Right
and Wrong, Truth and Reality**, War**, Wealth
and Poverty, Work*

French
Confidence, Greatness, Freedom, Greatness, Love

German
Character

Greek
Friendship

Haitian
Language and Words

Hasidic (Jewish)
Cooperation and Unity

Hausa (African)
Problems and Solutions

Indian
Good Fortune and Misfortune

Irish
Beauty, Home

Italian
*Effort and Enthusiasm, The Future, Happiness and
Sorrow, Success*

Japanese
Food**, Helping and Kindness, Success

Jewish
Problems and Solutions

Korean
Time

Latin
Experience, Greatness, Justice and Equality, Time

Mayan
Family

Malay
Self-Knowledge and Self-Respect

Mescalero Apache
Youth

Mexican
Beginnings and Endings, Change, Family, Good Fortune and Misfortune

Panamanian
Problems and Solutions

Persian
Wealth and Poverty

Russian
Friendship and Loyalty, Health, Leaders and Leadership

Scottish
Friendship and Loyalty, Wealth and Poverty

Somalian (African)
Family

Spanish
Wealth and Poverty

Swahili (African)
Work

Swedish
Manners

Welsh
Health

Winnebago
Nature

West African
Music

Wolof West African
Education and Learning

Venezuelan
Friendship and Loyalty

Vietnamese
Effort and Enthusiasm

Yiddish (Jewish)
Community and City Life

Yoruban (African)
Beauty

PUBLILIUS SYRUS (1ST CENTURY B.C.)
Latin actor remembered for his mime plays, in which he acted out sayings, each of which taught a lesson. He arrived in Rome as a slave, but soon was given his freedom. Because scholars used his name to record his words, he is known as the author of what became famous Latin sayings, called maxims, told in verse form. His name means Publilius the Syrian, possibly reflecting the land of his birth.
Happiness and Sorrow, Justice and Equality

PUTNAM, ISRAEL (1718–1790)
American Colonial military leader who served in the French and Indian War and later joined the Revolutionary forces around Boston, serving as commander general of the Continental forces at Bunker Hill.
*War***

PYLE, ERNIE (1900–1945)

U.S. war correspondent who became famous for his newspaper columns, which revealed the lives of ordinary soldiers during World War II. He traveled with the troops, sharing their hardships, and was killed during the Okinawa campaign.
Health

PYTHAGORAS (C. 582–500 B.C.)

Greek philosopher and mathematician who was interested in showing how numbers could be used to describe the proportions found in the natural world and in art. He left no writings, but his students and followers recorded his teachings.
Advice

RALEGH, SIR WALTER (C. 1552–1618)

British courtier, explorer, and poet who was a favorite of Queen Elizabeth I. He sent several expeditions to America, choosing the name Virginia for the southern coastal lands his settlers explored in honor of Elizabeth, who was called "the Virgin Queen." Although he spelled his last name as shown above, many historians refer to him as Raleigh.
Love and Hate

RANDOLPH, A. PHILIP (1889–1979)

U.S. labor leader and founder of the Brotherhood of Sleeping Car Porters who played a key role in the struggle for civil rights for African-Americans from the 1920s through the 1960s. He helped organize the march on Washington, D. C., where Martin Luther King, Jr., gave his now famous "I Have a Dream" speech. His full name was Asa Philip Randolph.
Freedom, Government and Politics

RANKIN, JEANETTE (1880–1973)

U.S. Congressperson and the first woman ever to serve in the U.S. House of Representatives. She served two terms, representing Montana from 1917–1919 and from 1941–1943. She was strongly opposed to all war and was the only member of the House to vote against the declarations of both World War I (1917) and World War II (1941). She also protested against U.S. involvement in the Vietnam War.
War

REAGAN, NANCY (B. 1923)

First lady of the U.S., she married Ronald Reagan when they were both actors working in Hollywood. As first lady, Nancy Reagan launched a campaign to get young people to "just say, 'no'" to drugs.
Health

REAGAN, RONALD (B. 1911)

Fortieth president of the United States, who was a popular film star before he entered politics. He was elected governor of California in 1966 and held that office until 1975. He served as president from 1981 to 1989.
Government and Politics

RENAULT, MARY (1905–1983)

South African novelist who was born in England. She won acclaim for her historical novels, which bring to life the culture of ancient Greece.
Self-Knowledge and Self-Respect

RICE, GRANTLAND (1880–1954)

U.S. sportswriter whose column "The Sportlight" appeared in newspapers all across the U.S.
Sports

RICHARDS, ANN (B. 1933)

Former governor of Texas known for her quick wit, determination, and strong opinions. In 1992 she served as chairperson of the Democratic National Convention.
Change, Humor

RICKENBACKER, EDDIE (1890–1973)

U.S. fighter pilot who was awarded the Medal of Honor in recognition of his efforts as commander of the 94th Aero Pursuit Squadron. After the war, he worked for automobile and airplane manufacturers. In 1943 he undertook a special flight for the U.S. government and was forced down over the Pacific. He and six of his seven crew members survived for 23 days on rubber rafts. He later described their ordeal and rescue in the book *Seven Came Through*.
Courage

RINEHART, MARY ROBERTS (1876–1958)

U.S. writer who was known for her suspenseful novels and plays that mix horror and humor. Many of her novels are mysteries in which a clever heroine narrates the book, narrowly misses great danger, and solves the crime.
Good Fortune and Misfortune

RIVERA, DIEGO (1886–1957)

Mexican painter whose powerful paintings and murals often reflected Mexican history and culture or made statements about political and social concerns. He was married to Frida Kahlo, another noted Mexican painter.
Art

ROBINSON, JACKIE (1919–1972)

U.S. baseball player and civil rights leader who became the first African-American to play major league baseball when he joined the Brooklyn Dodgers in 1947. He is also remembered for his skill at second base and his excellent batting record. He was elected to the Baseball Hall of Fame in 1962.
Sports

ROCHESTER, LORD (1647–1680)

British poet who was a leader of the "court wits" in the court of King Charles II. His full name and title was John Wilmot, Earl of Rochester.
Compliments and Insults

RODIN, AUGUSTE (1840–1917)

French sculptor whose bronze and marble sculptures are known for their realism. Rodin carefully modeled his figures out of wax and clay, and his assistants would then translate his work into metal or stone. His famous works include *The Thinker* and *The Kiss*.
Beauty

ROGERS, WILL (1879–1935)

U.S. humorist and entertainer of European and Cherokee descent who began his career doing rope tricks in Wild West shows and vaudeville

houses. He went on to star in movies and write a syndicated newspaper column. He also published several books that presented his unique slant on everyday life and politics.
*Human Nature**, News and the Media*

ROLAND, MADAME (1754–1793)
French revolutionary who was a political advisor and hostess for a political group called the Girondists during the early years of the French Revolution. However, when the Girondists and the Jacobins struggled for power and the Jacobins won, she was condemned to death and guillotined. Her full name was Jeanne Manon Phlipon Roland de la Platière.
Freedom

ROMULO, CARLOS PEÑA (1899–1985)
Philippine military leader and government official who worked as a journalist before he entered politics. He was one of the 51 founding members of the United Nations.
Justice and Equality

ROONEY, ANDY (B. 1919)
U.S. journalist who, as a commentator on the television show *60 Minutes,* shares his opinions about what he likes and doesn't like about everyday life. He has also published his commentaries in book form.
Creativity and Ideas

ROOSEVELT, ELEANOR (1884–1962)
First lady and human rights advocate whose active role in helping people in need earned her the title "first lady of the world." A niece of Theodore Roosevelt, she married a distant cousin, Franklin Delano Roosevelt, in 1905. As first lady, she spoke out to end discrimination and for the needs of the disadvantaged. After her husband's death, she served as U.S. delegate to the United Nations. In 1961 she chaired President Kennedy's Commission on the Status of Women.
*Change, Courage, Responsibility**, Self-Knowledge and Self-Respect, Youth*

ROOSEVELT, FRANKLIN DELANO (1882–1945)
Thirty-second president of the United States, who led the nation through the difficult years of the Great Depression and World War II. He was the only president elected four times. In 1921 Roosevelt was stricken by polio and throughout the rest of his life his ability to walk was hampered by the effects of this disease.
Advice, Courage, Happiness and Sorrow

ROOSEVELT, THEODORE (1858–1919)
Twenty-sixth president of United States, who became president when William McKinley was assassinated. He aimed to make the U.S. a leader among nations and at home instituted reforms to control the power of big business. He was also known for his athletic lifestyle, and he enjoyed being in the public eye. People called him "our Teddy."
*Character, Leaders and Leadership**, Wisdom, Work*

ROSSETTI, CHRISTINA (1830–1894)
British poet who was born in London and lived a quiet, religious life. She wrote poetry for children as well as religious verses. Her

brother, Dante Rossetti, was also a well-known poet and painter.
Family, Nature

ROUSSEAU, JEAN JACQUES (1712–1778)
French philosopher who was born in Geneva, Switzerland. He expressed his views in both the nonfiction and the fiction he wrote. He believed that people were shaped by society and by what they were taught. He said government must have the consent of the people. His most famous works include *The Social Contract* and *Emile.*
Experience, Nature, War

RUMI (1207–1273)
Persian Sufi teacher and poet known for his spiritual verses. He often danced while reciting his poetry. After his death his disciples became known in the West as whirling Dervishes. His full name was Jalal ad-Din ar-Rumi.
Envy and Jealousy

RUTH, BABE (1895–1948)
U.S. baseball player who in his 22 seasons as a major-leaguer hit 714 home runs. Babe Ruth was elected into the Baseball Hall of Fame in 1936. His full name was George Herman Ruth.
Sports

SADAT, ANWAR AL- (1918–1981)
Egyptian president and Nobel Peace Prize recipient. Under Sadat's leadership, Egypt negotiated with Israel to end the longtime conflict between the two countries. He was killed by religious militants who opposed his policies and his willingness to make peace with Israel.
Change, Peace

SAGAN, CARL (1934–1996)
U.S. astronomer, author, and educator who became famous when he wrote and narrated the television series *Cosmos.* In addition to writing about space, Sagan also wrote about the human brain in a book called *The Dragons of Eden,* for which he received the 1978 Pulitzer Prize in general nonfiction; he continued this theme with *Broca's Brain,* published in 1979.
Creativity and Ideas

SAIKAKU, IHARA SEE IHARA SAIKAKU

ST. AUGUSTINE SEE AUGUSTINE, SAINT

ST. CATHERINE OF SIENA SEE CATHERINE OF SIENA, SAINT

ST. DENIS, RUTH (1879–1968)
U.S. dancer and teacher who developed new forms of dance inspired by her study of traditional Asian dances. She began her career as a vaudeville and musical comedy performer. She formed her own school in 1915 with her husband and dance partner, Ted Shawn. She worked to create dances that expressed what she called "the noblest thoughts of man."
Dance

SANDBURG, CARL (1878–1967)
U.S. poet who also wrote histories and biographies as well as stories for children. He was strongly opposed to war and wrote several

antiwar poems. Sandburg also won acclaim for his six-volume history about Lincoln and the Civil War.
Dreams and Goals, Mathematics, War

SANTAYANA, GEORGE (1863–1952)
Spanish-American philosopher and poet. He moved to the U.S. in 1872 but retained his Spanish citizenship. He taught philosophy at Harvard University and published a number of books of verse and philosophy.
History

SARTON, MAY (1912–1995)
U.S. poet and journalist who was born in Belgium. In addition to writing poetry, she also published fiction and autobiographical memoirs including *A Journal of Solitude.*
Courage

SAWYER, DIANE (B. 1945)
U.S. television reporter and journalist who began her career as a weather reporter in Louisville, Kentucky, in 1967. She moved on to Washington, D. C., where she worked as a press secretary for President Richard Nixon. When Nixon left office, she spent several years working on his collected papers. In 1978 she became a reporter for the CBS news magazine *60 Minutes* and since then has moved on to ABC, where she anchors the show *PrimeTime Live.*
Effort and Enthusiasm

SCHOMBURG, ARTHUR A. (1874–1938)
U.S. historian who founded the Negro Society for Social Research. He was born and raised in Puerto Rico. As a boy who loved history and culture, he was disappointed when he could find little information about the history of people of African descent, and began collecting such material on his own. He came to New York in 1891. He worked in law and business and continued to build his collection of books and to write about the role of blacks in world history. His extensive collection served as the foundation for the Schomburg Center for Research in Black Culture, which is located in New York City.
Prejudice

SCHROEDER, PATRICIA (B. 1940)
U.S. politician who served in Congress, representing the state of Colorado from 1973 until 1996. In Congress she was a strong advocate for women's rights, civil rights, and gun control. She now serves as president of the Association of American Publishers.
War

SCHULZ, CHARLES (B. 1922)
U.S. creator of the cartoon *Peanuts,* which uses the characters Charlie Brown, a born loser and worrier, his dog Snoopy, and friends Linus, Lucy, and others to reveal the humor in the problems people encounter in everyday life. Schulz says that he based most of Charlie Brown's character on his own childhood experiences.
Ability and Talent, Family, Happiness and Sorrow

SCOTT, SIR WALTER (1771–1832)
Scottish poet and novelist whose works include the historical novel *Ivanhoe* and the long story poem *The Lady of the Lake.* Much of his writing reflects his beliefs that people of all

classes and from all cultures and religions can lead a good life and contribute to the betterment of the world.
Citizenship and Patriotism, Experience, Truth and Reality

SEATTLE, CHIEF (C. 1786–1866)
Suquamish and Dwamish leader whose speech to the Governor of Washington Territory in 1853 has become well-known. Seattle was a Christian and wanted to live peacefully with the whites.
Nature

SEEGER, PETE (B. 1919)
U.S. songwriter and folksinger who is known for his concern for social and environmental issues.
Music

SEI SHŌNAGON (966–1013)
Japanese poet and diarist who was in the service of the Empress Sadako. Sei is remembered for her work *Pillow Book*, an account of life in the imperial court.
Loneliness and Solitude

SENECA, LUCIUS ANNAEUS (C. 4 B.C.–A.D. 65)
Spanish-born Roman philosopher, author, and statesman who was called Seneca the Younger; his father was called Seneca the Elder. Seneca the Younger was born into a distinguished family and was active in political and literary life in Rome. He served as the tutor and advisor for the boy who would grow up to be Emperor Nero. Seneca wrote plays and philosophical essays, among other works.

Many of his letters also have survived to enlighten historians about Roman life.
Education and Learning, Language and Words

SERVICE, ROBERT (1874–1958)
Canadian poet known for his poems about life in the Yukon Territory during the gold rush days. His best known poems are "The Shooting of Dan McGrew" and "The Cremation of Sam McGee." Service was born in England, grew up in Scotland, and moved to Canada in 1894, settling in the Yukon in 1902. He left the Yukon in 1912 and traveled to many other places. He also wrote verse on other subjects as well as six novels.
Time

SEUSS, DR. (1904–1991)
U.S. author known for creating *The Cat in the Hat* and many other stories for children told in playful rhyme. Seuss illustrated his own work, inventing strange characters and landscapes. Some of his books, such as *Oh, the Places You'll Go* and *You're Only Old Once!*, appeal to adults as well. His real name was Theodor Seuss Geisel.
Choices, Education and Learning

SHAKESPEARE, WILLIAM (1564–1616)
British playwright and poet who is one of the most read and most quoted authors in the entire world. He wrote at least 37 plays, both comedies and tragedies, including the classics, *Macbeth* and *Hamlet*. Critics say that Shakespeare has remained popular for centuries because his work reveals a deep understanding of how people think and act. His use of language is full of clever

comparisons and rhythms; he even invented new words as it suited him to express his ideas.

Advice, Beauty, Envy and Jealousy, Family Greatness, Happiness and Sorrow, Humor, Language and Words**, Leaders and Leadership, Manners, Music, Truth and Reality

SHAW, GEORGE BERNARD (1856–1950)
Irish playwright who was born in Dublin but lived most of his life in London. In addition to writing over 50 plays, including *Pygmalion* and *Saint Joan,* Shaw was also an essayist, critic, and a founding member of the Fabian Society, a group of British intellectuals who published essays presenting their views about religion, government, and society.
Dreams and Goals

SHAW, HENRY WHEELER SEE BILLINGS, JOSH

SHELLEY, MARY WOLLSTONECRAFT (1797–1851)
British author who wrote the famous horror novel *Frankenstein* in 1818. Named Mary Wollstonecraft Godwin at birth, she was the daughter of author Mary Wollstonecraft, who wrote about women's rights, and minister and philospher William Godwin. In 1816 she married the great poet Percy Bysshe Shelley. After his death in 1822, she wrote several novels to support herself and her children.
Dreams and Goals

SHELLEY, PERCY BYSSHE (1792–1822)
British poet who is considered to be one of the greatest poets of the Romantic era. Among his most famous works are *Prometheus Unbound* and *Adonais*. In 1811 he married Harriet Westbrook and after her death in 1816 he married Mary Wollstonecraft Godwin, who wrote the famous horror novel *Frankenstein*.
Music

SHERMAN, WILLIAM TECUMSEH (1820–1891)
U.S. general remembered for his role as a general of Union troops during the Civil War. In 1864 Sherman led the army that captured Atlanta, Georgia, and burned part of the city. His troops continued on through the Carolinas, burning and destroying property in their path. From 1869–1883 Sherman served as commanding General of the U.S. Army.
War

SHŌNAGON SEI SEE SEI SHŌNAGON

SINGER, ISAAC BASHEVIS (1904–1991)
Polish-American author who wrote in Yiddish. He was the son of a rabbi and was educated in a rabbinical school in Poland. He came to the U.S. in 1935 and many of his works first appeared in the *Jewish Daily Forward*, a New York Yiddish-language newspaper. In addition to his many books for adults, he also wrote stories for children. In 1978 he won the Nobel Prize in Literature.
Truth and Reality, Writing

SMITH, ALFRED (1873–1944)
U.S. politician who was elected governor of New York four times and was the first Roman Catholic to run for president. Smith was largely self-educated. He left school at the age

of twelve to work as a newsboy. He then spent seven years working in the Fulton Fish Market in New York City.
Compliments and Insults

Socrates (469–399 B.C.)

Greek philosopher and teacher whose famous pupils included the philosopher Plato and the historian Xenephon. He believed that evil and wrong actions are caused by ignorance. He devoted himself to searching for truth and goodness and to teaching. He taught in public places, presenting ideas and then questioning his listeners in a way that led them to reason out logical answers to his questions. Socrates taught his pupils not to accept everything that their rulers did without question; he even questioned who should rule. For this he was considered dangerous and was sentenced to death.
Citizenship and Patriotism, Creativity and Ideas**, Friendship and Loyalty

Solzhenitsyn, Alexander (b. 1918)

Russian author known for his novels, which reflect his experiences during World War II, the years he spent as a political prisoner in Soviet labor camps, and the years he spent in exile. He received the Nobel Prize in Literature in 1970.
Animals, Justice and Equality

Soong Mei-Ling (Madame Chiang Kai-shek) (1901–1987)

Chinese political reformer and educator who was married to the Chinese Nationalist leader Chiang Kai-shek. She became an eloquent spokesperson for the Chinese Nationalist government in the 1940s and 1950s.
Character

Spyri, Johanna (1827–1901)

Swiss author of *Heidi*, a classic novel for children that tells how an independent little girl changes the life of the people she meets when she comes to live with her grandfather in the mountains. Spyri also wrote other books for children as well as short stories for adults.
Anger

St. (last names beginning with) see SAINT

Standing Bear, Luther (1868–1939)

Oglala Sioux writer and leader who was one of the best-known Native American authors of his time. He used his writing to record and preserve traditional values of his culture.
Manners, Prejudice

Stanton, Elizabeth Cady (1815–1902)

U.S. advocate for women's rights who, with Lucretia Mott, organized the first woman's right's convention in the U.S. The meeting was held in Stanton's hometown, Seneca Falls, New York, in 1848. At the meeting Stanton presented a Declaration of Sentiments that she had written using the Declaration of Independence as a model. In 1851 she met Susan B. Anthony, and they began to work together for their common goals. During the 1850s and 1860s they worked for the abolition of slavery as well as for the rights of

women. In 1869 Stanton was elected president of the National Woman Suffrage Association.
Change, Family, Leaders and Leadership

STEVENSON, ROBERT LOUIS (1850–1894)
Scottish author whose famous works include *Kidnapped, Treasure Island, A Child's Garden of Verses,* and *The Strange Case of Dr. Jekyll and Mr. Hyde.* He was an extremely versatile writer, creating historical adventure novels, poetry, eerie fantasy stories, and realistic fiction and nonfiction based on his travels. Although he always suffered from poor health, Stevenson traveled throughout Europe, America, and the South Seas. He spent his last years in Samoa.
Books and Reading, Language and Words

STONE, LUCY (1818–1893)
U.S. campaigner for women's rights who also lectured on the evils of slavery. In 1855 she married Henry Blackwell, but elected to keep her own name after marriage; she was probably the first woman to do so, and other married women who followed her example were called Lucy Stoners. In 1869 she helped establish the American Woman's Suffrage Society and founded the group's newspaper.
Prejudice, Work

SULLIVAN, ANNE (1866–1936)
Irish-born U.S. educator who is remembered as the dedicated teacher of Helen Keller. Keller was both blind and deaf. Sullivan devised special techniques adapted from those used by her educators to teach the girl to communicate with sign language, read braille, and even speak. Sullivan herself had had severe vision problems as a child and had been educated at the Perkins Institute for the Blind.
Education and Learning

SULLIVAN, LOUIS HENRI (1856–1924)
U.S. architect who was known for the originality of his designs and his philosophy. He believed that the structure of a building must reflect both society and nature.
Nature

SWIFT, JONATHAN (1667–1745)
Irish-born English author remembered as the author of the classic *Gulliver's Travels* and for his skill as an essayist with a talent for humor and satire. He was born in Dublin to English parents and throughout his life was deeply concerned about the welfare of both lands and the behavior of the English toward Ireland. He was an Anglican priest but also maintained an active interest in politics. He wrote many articles in support of Tory politics. In 1713, in recognition of his political work, Queen Anne named him dean of St. Patrick's Cathedral in Dublin.
Books and Reading, Creativity and Ideas, Health, Old Age

SYRUS, PUBLILIUS SEE PUBLILIUS SYRUS

TACITUS (C. A.D. 56–C. A.D. 120)
Roman historian who was also known for his skill as a speaker and politician. His *Histories* and *Annals* are very critical of the emperors whose reigns he describes. He believed that rulers should be elected and not receive their

right to govern by birth. His full name was Cornelius Tacitus.
War

TAGORE, RABINDRANATH (1861–1941)
Indian writer and philosopher who wrote in the Bengali language. He won the 1913 Nobel Prize in Literature. In 1901 he established a school based upon his philosophy, which tried to blend the best of Hindu and Western culture. He was a gifted composer and set many of his own poems to music. He also supported India's struggle for independence from Great Britain.
Effort and Enthusiasm, Leaders and Leadership, Old Age

TAN, AMY (B. 1952)
U.S. author who won acclaim for her novels, including *The Joy Luck Club* and *The Hundred Secret Senses,* which tell of family relationships and Chinese-American culture. She is also the author of two books for children, *The Moon Lady* and *The Chinese Siamese Cats.*
Food

TCHAIKOVSKY, PYOTR ILICH (1840–1893)
Russian composer whose music combines Russian traditions with the traditions of Western Europe. His orchestral pieces are played in concert halls around the world. He also wrote the music for several operas and ballets, including *Swan Lake* and *The Nutcraker.*
Music

TENNYSON, LORD ALFRED (1809–1892)
British poet who became the poet laureate, or official poet, of Great Britain in 1850, succeeding William Wordsworth. Tennyson was probably the most popular poet of his day. He was awarded the title of Baron by Queen Victoria in 1883. Many of his poems tell stories and give examples of the value of acting heroically when faced with difficult choices.
*Love and Hate, War***

TERESA, MOTHER (1910–1997)
Missionary, Roman Catholic nun, and Nobel Peace Prize winner. Born Agnes Goxha Bojaxhiu, in what used to be Albania, she grew up hearing stories about Jesuit missionaries and the work they did in India. By the time she was twelve she knew that she wanted to become a missionary. She began her mission work in India as a teacher and then as school principal. In 1946 she established a mission in Calcutta to aid the sick and the homeless. Under her leadership, her religious order, the Missionaries of Charity, became an official Catholic religious community of more than 700 nuns and 100 brothers, serving the poor in 87 countries.
Action, Loneliness and Solitude

THATCHER, MARGARET (B. 1925)
British prime minister who served from 1979 to 1990. She was the first woman ever to become prime minister. She worked to reduce government control over the nation's economy. Before entering politics, she worked as a research chemist and then as a lawyer.
Success

THOMAS, DYLAN (1914–1953)

Welsh author known for his passionate poetry. He became popular by giving dramatic public readings of his works throughout Great Britain and the U.S. His most famous poems include "Fern Hill" and "Do Not Go Gentle into That Good Night." He also wrote humor, short stories, and plays.

Old Age

THOREAU, HENRY DAVID (1817–1862)

U.S. philosopher and author whose most famous work, *Walden, or Life in the Woods,* tells of the two years he spent living alone, close to nature, in a small hut on the shore of Walden Pond near Concord, Massachusetts. In addition, he published many essays which presented his beliefs. A number of books, including a 20-volume set of his collected works and letters, was published some years after his death. Thoreau opposed slavery and believed that people should be free to refuse to obey any law that they felt was unjust and that violated their sense of right and wrong. In 1846 he practiced what he called "passive resistance," spending the night in jail when he refused to pay taxes as a protest against slavery. Leo Tolstoy, Mohandas Gandhi, and Martin Luther King, Jr., were among the great reformers and leaders who cited Thoreau as an influence on their lives.

Animals, History, Home, Loneliness and Solitude, Prejudice, Travel and Adventure, Truth and Reality, Wealth and Poverty, Writing

TOLKIEN, J. R. R. (1892–1973)

South African-born British author of the fantasies *The Hobbit* and the trilogy *Lord of the Rings,* set in an imaginary kingdom called middle earth. His full name was John Ronald Reuel Tolkien and he taught medieval languages and literature at Oxford University. Scholars say that his middle earth stories reflect words and themes from medieval English, German, and Scandinavian languages and literature.

Curiosity

TOLSTOY, LEO (1828–1910)

Russian author whose full name is sometimes written as Leo Nikolaevich Tolstoi. He is considered to be one of the most important novelists in world literature. His two most famous books are *War and Peace* and *Anna Karenina.* In addition to his work as a writer, Tolstoy, who was born into a wealthy family and lived on a huge country estate, concerned himself with social and religious reforms. He opened a school to educate the children of peasants on his estate and later in his life he gave up all his property to live simply.

Family

TROLLOPE, ANTHONY (1815–1882)

British writer remembered as the popular author of more than 50 novels. His mother, Frances Trollope, was also a well-known author. Before he became a successful novelist, Trollope worked as a clerk in the post office. He designed the red mail boxes that are still used in England today.

Effort and Enthusiasm

TRUDEAU, PIERRE ELIOTT (B. 1919)

Canadian prime minister who led his nation from 1968–1979 and from 1980–1984. He

was the third French-Canadian in history to become prime minister. He worked to strengthen relations with other nations and to ease tensions at home between French-speaking and English-speaking Canadians.
Citizenship and Patriotism, Government and Politics

TRUMAN, HARRY S (1884–1972)

Thirty-third president of the United States, who had been vice president for only 83 days when, in 1945, President Franklin D. Roosevelt died and he had to assume the presidency. Known for his blunt, direct way of speaking, he led the nation during the concluding months of World War II, making the decision to use atomic warfare against Japan. After the war was over, he worked on programs to stimulate a peacetime economy. He also established foreign policies that took a strong stand supporting nations that were resisting communist aggression. In 1950 he sent forces to protect South Korea against North Korea when its Communist forces invaded South Korea.
Animals, Peace, Responsibility

TRUTH, SOJOURNER (C. 1797–1883)

U.S. human rights advocate and former slave in New York State who changed her name from Isabella Van Wagoner (at birth her last name was Baumfree, after her father). She traveled around the country speaking out for the rights of African-Americans and women. She used examples from her own life and quotations from the Bible to help her convince her audiences.
*Right and Wrong, Truth and Reality***

TUBMAN, HARRIET (C. 1820–1913)

U.S. abolitionist who was born a slave in Maryland and escaped to the North to secure her own freedom. She returned South 19 times to lead over 300 enslaved people to freedom. During the Civil War, she spied for the Union Army, nursed wounded and sick soldiers, served meals, and did whatever else she could. After the war was over, she continued to speak out for the rights of African-Americans and women.
Freedom

TUTU, DESMOND (B. 1931)

South African religious and civil rights leader who won the Nobel Peace Prize in 1984 for his nonviolent campaign against apartheid, the policy of racial segregation that was part of South African life until apartheid laws were repealed in 1990–1991. Tutu was ordained as an Anglican priest in 1961. In 1986 he became the first black to be elected archbishop of Cape Town.
Cooperation and Unity, Peace

TWAIN, MARK (1835–1910)

U.S. humorist and writer whose most famous works are *The Adventures of Tom Sawyer, The Adventures of Huckleberry Finn* and *Life on the Mississippi*. In the late 1850s, his love for travel led him to become a riverboat pilot. A few years later, he began working as a journalist and decided to sign his newspaper columns with the pen name Mark Twain instead of his real name, Samuel Langhorne Clemens. "Mark Twain" comes from an old riverboat term used to measure the depth of

the river. Twain is another way of saying two, and mark twain equals two fathoms (12 feet).
Books and Reading, Experience, Humor**, Language and Words, Right and Wrong, Success, Truth and Reality, Work

TYLER, ANNE (B. 1941)
U.S. author whose novels and short stories for adults focus on modern family life. Her novel *Breathing Lessons* won the Pulitzer Prize in fiction in 1989.
Good Fortune and Misfortune

VAN BUREN, ABIGAIL ("DEAR ABBY") (B. 1918)
U.S. newspaper columnist known as "Dear Abby." In her column she responds to letters from readers, offering common sense advice in plain language. Her real name is Pauline Friedman.
Character

VAN GOGH, VINCENT (1853–1890)
Dutch artist who is remembered for his paintings, which hang in museums all over Europe and the U.S. Yet van Gogh received so little recognition that he sold only one of his paintings during his lifetime. His use of bright colors and wide circular brush strokes make his paintings easy to recognize. During the last years of his life he struggled with mental illness. He cut off his own earlobe with a razor in 1888 and committed suicide less than two years later.
Dreams and Goals

VAN DER ROHE, LUDWIG MIES SEE MIES VAN DER ROHE, LUDWIG

VICTORIA (1819–1901)
Queen of the United Kingdom of Great Britain and Ireland, she became queen when she was just eighteen years old. She reigned for 63 years, the longest any British monarch has ever held the throne. She was a hard-working ruler and wise enough to understand that the times required a more democratic form of government. During her rule, reforms were passed that allowed Parliament more authority in running the nation. Britain also became a vast empire during her reign, including 25 percent of the world's land and population. India, Egypt, Australia, Canada, and many other lands were part of this powerful empire.
Self-Knowledge and Self-Respect, Success

VIRGIL (70–19 B.C.)
Roman poet whose full name was Publius Vergilius Maro. He wrote books of poetry, the most famous of which is the *Aenid*, an epic poem. It tells the story of the Trojan War and of Aeneas, a Trojan hero who survived the fall of Troy to the Greeks, sailed west to Italy, and formed a new nation. The *Aenid* continues to tell how Aeneas's descendants founded the city of Rome and about the great accomplishments Romans achieved over the years.
Ability and Talent

VOLTAIRE (1694–1778)
French writer and philosopher whose real name was François-Marie Arouet. His writing showed his sharp wit and his strong sense of right and wrong. Early in his career, his satires offended the government and got him imprisoned in the Bastille for 11 months. He kept writing and soon he was creating plays

that made him famous. He also wrote poetry, histories, and philosophical tales and letters. He traveled throughout Europe and had influence on Frederick the Great of Germany and Catherine the Great of Russia.
Freedom, Greatness

VOS SAVANT, MARILYN (B. 1946)
U.S. advice columnist whose I.Q. is 228, one of the highest ever recorded. Her weekly column "Ask Marilyn" appears in *Parade* magazine.
Choices

WALKER, MADAME C. J. (1867–1919)
U.S. business leader who became the first self-made woman millionaire in America and by 1910 was running the nation's largest African-American-owned business. She created the Walker system, hair care products that met the needs of black women. She soon branched out into cosmetics and other beauty products. Her original name was Sarah Breedlove.
Good Fortune and Misfortune

WALLACE, WILLIAM ROSS (1819–1881)
U.S. poet who is remembered for his poem "The Hand That Rules the World."
Family

WALTON, IZAAK (1593–1683)
British author who published biographies of leading figures but is best remembered as the author of *The Compleat Angler, or, The Contemplative Man's Recreation.* This work includes bits of verse, quotations, and descriptions of country scenery as well as information about fishing and hunting.
Health

WANG AN (1920–1990)
Chinese-born U.S. engineer and founder of a major computer company, he made his first breakthrough discovery about computer technology in the Harvard Computer Laboratory. In 1951 he founded Wang Laboratories, which was one of the most successful high-tech companies of its era.
Science and Technology

WANG FU-CHIH (1619–1692)
Chinese historian who served in the military, raising an army (1644–50) to help the Ming Dynasty resist the invasion of Mongol warriors. Later in life he devoted himself entirely to the study of history and philosophy. He wrote two major works of history and also wrote poetry.
Government and Politics

WARHOL, ANDY (1927–1987)
U.S. artist best known for his images of common objects like soup cans and portraits of famous people, including Marilyn Monroe. He said he got his inspiration from ads and other things on television and in print. He also worked in films.
Future

WARREN, MERCY OTIS (1728–1814)
American playwright and historian who spent 30 years writing a three-volume history of the American Revolution. She also wrote passionately about her concerns for the new

nation's Constitution. Her words helped convince the new leaders to add the Bill of Rights, 10 amendments or additions to the Constitution that further safeguard personal freedoms.
Government and Politics

WASHINGTON, BOOKER T. (1856–1915)
U.S. educator and civil rights leader who was born in slavery and became the most influential African-American leader of his time. He founded and ran the Tuskegee Institute, a school that educated and trained African-Americans to succeed in a variety of careers. He also advised presidents Theodore Roosevelt and William Taft on racial issues. He published his autobiography *Up from Slavery* in 1901.
Character, Friendship and Loyalty

WASHINGTON, GEORGE (1732–1799)
First president of the United States, who planned to live the life of a gentleman farmer until, as a member of the Virginia House of Burgesses, he became involved in politics and became one of the leaders of Colonial opposition to British policies in America. He went on to command the Continental Army. After the Colonies had won their independence, he served as president of the convention that wrote the Constitution. There was much popular support for crowning him king, but Washington refused this honor and instead became the first president, serving two terms before retiring from public life.
Character, Freedom, Manners, Peace, War

WASHINGTON, MARTHA (1731–1802)
American Colonist and 1st first lady of the U.S. who was a wealthy widow and the mother of two children before she married George Washington in 1759. Throughout the Revolutionary War and her husband's years as president, she moved from place to place to support her husband as needed and perform the duties her new role required. She was the first U.S. woman to have her portrait appear on paper money (1886) and on a stamp (1902).
Happiness and Sorrow

WEBSTER, DANIEL (1782–1852)
U.S. lawyer and statesman who gained fame for his eloquent speeches delivered in courtrooms and in Congress. He championed the idea of a strong, unified national government. After his death, some of his speeches were required reading in classrooms, especially in the Northern states.
Cooperation and Unity, Success, Truth and Reality

WHITE, E. B. (1899–1985)
U.S. writer who was known for his essays, poetry, and his classic children's books *Stuart Little, Charlotte's Web*, and *The Trumpet of the Swan.* Elwyn Brooks White was awarded a special Pulitzer Prize in 1978.
Humor, Government

WHITEHEAD, ALFRED NORTH (1861–1947)
British mathematician and philosopher remembered for his influential books, including *Process and Reality* (1929), in which he says that process and reality are the tools

people use to learn about nature, their own experiences, and even God. He also worked with another noted British mathematician-philosopher on another classic book called *Principia Mathematica*.
Mathematics

WHITMAN, WALT (1819–1892)
U.S. poet who worked as a schoolteacher and a journalist and at a variety of other jobs. During the Civil War, he worked as a volunteer in military hospitals. Because every publisher to which he submitted his work rejected it as too unusual, he published several editions of his now-famous collection of poems, *Leaves of Grass,* on his own between the years 1855–1882. In his poetry, Whitman celebrates both the individuality of each person and his or her unique contribution to the world and the connectedness of all people to each other and to nature.
Animals, Community and City Life, Nature

WILCOX, ELLA WHEELER (1850–1919)
U.S. poet who for many years wrote a daily poem that was published in many newspapers. This made her one of the most-read poets of her day. Her work was also collected and published in more than 20 books of poems. She also wrote fiction and essays.
Humor

WILDE, OSCAR (1854–1900)
Irish playwright and novelist who believed that style and wit were important in everyday life as well as in art. He believed that many people of his day were narrow-minded and he sometimes used what he wrote to challenge popular ideas. Most of his plays were comedies, but he is also remembered for his horror novel, *The Portrait of Dorian Gray*, and for his collection of original fairy tales, *The Happy Prince and Other Stories*.
Friendship and Loyalty

WILDER, THORNTON (1897–1975)
U.S. playwright and novelist remembered for his Pulitzer Prize-winning works, the plays *Our Town* and *The Skin of Our Teeth* and the novel *The Bridge of San Luis Rey*. In addition to several other plays and novels, he also published essays and other nonfiction.
Animals

WILLIAMS, BETTY (B. 1943)
Irish activist who was co-winner of the Nobel Prize for Peace in honor of her work creating a women's movement to end the violence in Northern Ireland. The Community for Peace People, an organization founded by Williams and Mairead Corrigan, called upon Catholics and Protestants to work together against terrorism and to promote tolerance.
Peace

WILLIAMS, HANK (1923–1953)
U.S. country-music singer and songwriter who taught himself to play the guitar when he was eight years old. At thirteen, he formed his own band, which soon began to perform in concerts and on the radio. In 1947 he moved to Nashville, Tennessee, and became famous for his performances at the Grand Ole Opry. He wrote over 100 songs before he died of a heart ailment at the age of twenty-nine.
Loneliness and Solitude

WILMOT, JOHN, EARL OF ROCHESTER
SEE ROCHESTER, LORD

WILSON, WOODROW (1856–1924)
Twenty-eighth president of the United States
whose full name was Thomas Woodrow
Wilson. He worked as a lawyer, teacher, and
university president before he entered politics
in 1910, when he successfully campaigned to
become governor of New Jersey. As president
he faced many challenges, including leading
the nation through World War I. He was
instrumental in drafting the Treaty of
Versailles, which ended the war in Europe.
He actively campaigned for the establishment
of the League of Nations, an international
organization intended to help nations settle
their differences without going to war.
Change, Peace

WINCHELL, WALTER (1897–1972)
U.S. journalist who dropped out of school at
the age of thirteen and worked onstage as a
vaudeville performer before he began writing
show business gossip for newspapers. His
columns and, later, his radio broadcasts
reached readers and listeners all over the
country.
Time

WINFREY, OPRAH (B. 1954)
U.S. television star who won fame for her daily
program, *The Oprah Winfrey Show*. Earlier in
her career she was the first African-American
in Nashville, Tennessee, to anchor the news.
She has won critical acclaim for her acting and

her best-selling books. She also runs her own
television and film production company.
Good Fortune and Misfortune, Prejudice

WOLLSTONECRAFT, MARY (1759–1797)
British advocate for women's rights who is
best-known for her book *A Vindication of the
Rights of Women*. Published in 1792, this
book was one of the first to propose that
women and men should have the same rights.
Wollstonecraft also stressed the importance
of providing a good education for girls as well
as for boys. In 1797 she married a political
reformer named William Godwin. Their
daughter, Mary Wollstonecraft Shelley, also
became an author; in 1818 she penned the
classic horror novel *Frankenstein*.
Justice and Equality

WOODSON, CARTER G. (1875–1950)
U.S. historian who founded the Association
for the Study of Negro Life and History and
its *Journal of Negro History*. Although his
parents were former slaves and he was unable
to receive any formal schooling until he was
twenty years old, Woodson went on to receive
B.A. and M.A. degrees from the University of
Chicago. He received a Ph.D. from Harvard
University in 1915. He is remembered as
"the father of Negro history" because of the
organization and journal he founded, as well as
the many books he published on this subject.
History

WORDSWORTH, WILLIAM (1770–1850)
English poet who became poet laureate,
or official poet, of Great Britain, in 1843.
He based most of his poetry on his own

experiences and feelings, often composing new lines and reciting them aloud to himself as he walked through the woods near his home. *Loneliness and Solitude*

WRIGHT, ORVILLE (1871–1948)
U.S. inventor who, working with his brother Wilbur, achieved the first successful flight in a motor-powered airplane (1903). The Wright brothers began as bicycle manufacturers and experimented with kites and gliders before they began working on airplanes. *Science and Technology, Travel and Adventure*

WU CHEN (1280–1354)
Chinese painter who was known for his depictions of landscapes and fisherman at work. He is remembered as one of the Four Masters of the Yuan Dynasty. *Art*

YEATS, WILLIAM BUTLER (1865–1939)
Irish poet and playwright who also translated ancient Gaelic folktales into English. He won the Nobel Prize in Literature in 1923. Irish history, legend, and locales figured prominently in his writing. *Education and Learning*

YUTANG, LIN SEE LIN YUTANG

ZAPATA, EMILIANO (C. 1877–1919)
Mexican revolutionary whose main goal was to regain land for his people, the descendants of the Native Americans who lived in Mexico long before the Spanish arrived. With Pancho Villa, he invaded Mexico City in 1919. *Peace*

About the Author

ADRIENNE BETZ is a writer, editor, and educator who specializes in children's books and curriculum materials. She began her career as a children's librarian in New York and Pennsylvania. During the past twenty years, she has helped develop reading, language arts, and social studies textbooks for several major educational publishers. She has published anthologies of short stories, poetry, and folktales and lectures on issues relating to children's literature.

Compiling the quotations for this book took several years of research, but Ms. Betz says that she had been collecting quotations long before she began researching this book:

"When I was a child, my father read to me. Of course, most of the books we shared were storybooks borrowed from the children's section of the library. However, my father also shared his love of literature in another way. He always had a wonderful memory for strings of words that stood alone. He would pull a book from the shelf and read aloud sentences so powerful that they made noble and surprising new ideas spring to life. This was my first introduction to quotations. I knew of William Shakespeare, Mark Twain, Ralph Waldo Emerson, Winston Churchill, Henry Wadsworth Longfellow and many other fine writers long before I was able to read or understand their full works, because my father quoted them—often.

Many of the quotations my father shared with me so long ago are now part of this book. I also followed my father's example when I began reading on my own—especially when I did research for this book. I looked for those shining sentences—the kind that leap out and beg to be written down and remembered."